THE FAMILY OF GOD

EXPERIENCING CHURCH AS FAMILY

Sea Hill Press Inc.

THE FAMILY OF GOD

EXPERIENCING CHURCH AS FAMILY

Jason Lomelino, Lucas Bell
& the IV Church Family

SEA·HILL
PRESS

Sea Hill Press Inc.
www.seahillpress.com
Santa Barbara, California
Book design by Walter Sharp

Cover design by Jacob Reeve
Photography by Janelle Stephanie Bosko

ISBN: 978-1-937720-13-1

Printed in the United States of America

WE INVITE YOU TO FOLLOW OUR VIDEOS OF
GOD'S WORK IN OUR FAMILY AND CITY AT
WWW.JESUSLOVESIV.COM

CONTENTS

FOREWORD

Simply put, the government of God is family. There is a Father seated next to a husband, who is coming for His bride. We are the bride, but we are also children of the Father. I know this is starting to sound like some crazy love triangle or something, but it is actually the Kingdom. See, you aren't the bride by gender, but by position. You are the target for all the affections of the husband, Jesus. You have His heart and He hopes to have yours. But you are also God's children, His sons actually. Men, you are still a part of the bride; and women, you are also sons. Why? Because sons had the greatest inheritance in the family. They would not only receive the joy of working with the Father but also a portion of all He saved just for them. We are God's children and we are the Son's bride. Everything in Christianity functions from these core realities about our identity. It's all about relationship and it begins with your relationship to God.

Should be pretty straightforward from there, right?

I wish.

I have been married for over ten years now, and we have three kids, yet I still feel like I know nothing about relationships. I have met couples married over fifty years who say the same thing. In marriage, you are always learning; the day you aren't, you're either dead or divorced. We are all trying to understand the dynamics of relationships, spending thousands on therapy every year to talk about ourselves in hopes that we will figure this thing out. But alas, there is no goal or great "aha" moment where you arrive and know everything. Like all the best parts of life, it is the journey that gives us the greatest glimpse of beauty and the hope that things will continue to get better than they are today.

I don't know what you were expecting as you picked up this book. Perhaps you are a leader trying to learn how to do things a little different in your church, maybe you have a small group on a campus and are looking for a few new ideas, or maybe you've heard about Jesus Burgers and the IV crew and are just looking for some cool stories. Whatever your reasoning, you need to lay it down and prepare yourself for what is in the following pages. This is not a how-to book, nor is it a step-by-step plan for developing a community in a college town. These are stories of sacrifice and triumph, failure and heartbreak—all of which form bonds that can either last a lifetime or divide you from the start.

Real relationships take courage, sacrifice, and humility. Many people are merely looking for the next good meeting and the next hip church they can attend. Let me tell you what I think God wants: He wants to destroy all your perceptions about what relationships look like and what they cost; He wants you to examine your heart and with the help of the Holy Spirit root out selfishness and pride, two of the most destructive forces in relationships; and He wants to help build a new foundation so that when the waves of the world crash against the foundations of your friendships and marriages, you are left standing firm for others to see. It is going to be healing for many of us to talk about the guilt we have in relationships and to finally yell at the top of our lungs, "I suck at this, somebody please help me!" Okay, maybe that's just me. But I will tell you what, when I found mothers and fathers to help me I learned that I can trust and love with reckless abandon and without fear of rejection mucking up the place.

I know there is hope for the world when I see marriages that last and parents who don't give up on their kids. This is the Kingdom, the beautiful expression of heaven on earth. It looks like a man and woman choosing each other for life, having children, and teaching them that all they ever need is found in the source of true love, the man who sacrificed himself for all, Jesus. In that same love, children must be allowed to make mistakes without feeling like failures and to experience triumphs without fear of not meeting their parent's expectations. Teaching them about sex and purity and helping them adjust to a world of make-believe romance is necessary, not only with words, great verses, and bumbling theologies, but with actual experiences and all of life's imperfections. Only this will show children that it is okay for you to be exactly you. You, with your bumps, bruises, and scars, are making a way for someone else to do it better.

Now that I think about it, maybe why you really picked up this book is because at the end of the day, all we really want is someone to help us do life a little bit better.

I join you and all the others on this journey. Let's be seekers forever in the great ocean of His love.

Thanks to everyone who penned and bled to make this story happen; yours is a true testimony of love.

Jake Hamilton,
Jesus Culture Music Artist

INTRODUCTION

From eternity past, God has always been Father and will always be Father. The cross of Christ opened the door for all of God's sons and daughters to come home to Him and experience the life they were created for. Family was never just a human idea; it originated in the heart of God. It was part of His eternal purpose that He had in mind when He created us and gave us desires that could only be fulfilled in communion with Him and with others. Without family, we cannot step into the fullness of our destiny in Jesus or who we were created to be in life.

In over a decade of pastoring a church mostly comprised of people under the age of thirty, I have noticed that those who have embraced the family of God are those who have continued to mature in Christ and produce fruit that remains. The younger generation today is hungry for family, community, and life together. Young people will spend hours upon hours on social media platforms longing to connect with, and feel a part of, something greater than themselves. Deep down we all know there is more. We know we were created with a purpose, to do great things for the Kingdom of God. I believe that what we all long to discover becomes unlocked once we embrace God's plan of doing life together with others.

The modern world teaches us to build fortresses around our lives, homes, and hearts to keep people out of them. In contrast, God, who is all knowing and good, has created us to invite people into our lives.

Psalm 68:6 says, "God sets the lonely in families." The Bible is clear that real joy is found in fellowship with God and one another (1 John 1:1-3). For over ten years now my wife and I have lived in a city of over twenty thousand people in one square mile. For two and a half years of those ten, we lived in a house of over twenty people who were part of our church. We served as the house dad and mom. Not surprisingly, we had no clue what we were signing up for. The home we live in today with our four young children, the oldest age eight, has hundreds of people who visit and come through it every year. These people come for church, for meetings, for counsel, or to live life with us. While we absolutely love the life we have been called to, we recognize it is unique, and we are in no way advocating that everyone needs to live their lives like ours. However, we firmly believe that God's heart is that we would all be involved in some type of covenant community where we are known and where we know others. His purposes in the earth are far bigger than our own individual capabilities. My faith is not enough. Your faith is not enough. We need *our* faith.

If we are not careful, we can easily treat church more like a restaurant than a family. We come only to get what we want and leave a tip (tithe). That is not family; that is consumerism. Family is called to sacrifice for one another as Christ sacrificed for us (1 John 3:16). Family is about preferring one another and fighting for each other's dreams. The life Jesus demonstrated was one of sacrificial love for all people, especially those of the household of faith (Galatians 6:10).

The IVC family does not view church as a place to go to; it views church as a family to belong to. This book and its stories are not intended to give a personal preference for how to do church. Our intention is to release a simple truth: the church is a family.

Jesus told us that the world will know us by our love for one another. God wants to form more covenantal families, places where His children are committed to one another and ultimately to Him. Church history shows us that people tend to look for better structures, while in the Bible God focuses on love: His love for us, our love for Him, our love for one another, and ultimately our love for the world. This book is not a list of dos and don'ts for a successful church, nor is it a book on church theory. Instead, it is a book that highlights some of our family values that have produced life in God and fruit that remains.

Many churches are tempted to measure success by money and attendance. God, however, measures it by love (John 15). What we have seen in the Isla Vista Church family is that love for Jesus and His Kingdom naturally causes us to love one another. It has always begun with Jesus and His heart for our city that we are called to love. We realized along the way that for this to work in the city of Isla Vista it must first work in our church family.

This book is about real people who chose family, and as a result, experienced radical life transformation from God. Family is a choice. While it can be hard and sometimes messy, it is one of God's most beautiful blessings He could give us. For me, it took a church family to discover the truth that we need others to grow up in Christ, to learn from, and to extend the Kingdom of God with. God's desire for family is hidden in each of us, and I trust that this book will stir this desire in your heart and give you a practical look at how to build the family of God wherever you are.

In Christ,
Jason Lomelino

1

Community Living

"Love each other with genuine affection, and
take delight in honoring each other."

—Romans 12:10 (NLT)

COMMUNITY LIVING

JASON LOMELINO

Anyone who has ever experienced living in community knows that it takes God to love and continue to love the people you are living life with. God hardwired each of us for community, for we are made in the image of God, who is community within Himself. The heart of God is for each of His children to live in community with the Godhead and one another. His desire has been well articulated in the beginning of 1 John, "What we have seen and heard we proclaim to you also, so that you too may have fellowship with us; and indeed our fellowship is with the Father, and with His Son Jesus Christ. These things we write, so that our joy may be made complete." When the church has fellowship with God and one another, we experience the completion of joy. Joy is unlocked in our hearts when we choose to no longer live separately from others but rather to pursue a life of community with God and one another. Community living allows for us to have the daily experience of real fellowship centered on God, teaching us to love His family.

Community is not simply living in the same house as other people. Many people can live in the same house but not actually know each other or even care to know each other. People often tend to go about their daily lives apart from one another, failing to include others in matters of the heart and personal details. Living with people is one thing; but sharing the experiences of life and living intentionally with each other is a completely different mindset.

A simple definition of community is common-unity. The common-unity of a Christian community is surprisingly not the same theology or ecclesiology; it is merely the person of Jesus. He alone fosters and creates genuine community, as individuals desire to keep Him the center of their lives.

Relationships teach us to love, while circumstances and situations teach us to trust. As a pastor, I have always leaned toward application when sharing a word rather than imparting straight knowledge. Sermons can often make us feel as if we have accomplished something, when really we have only heard something. Reading a book on community or even studying the Book of Acts will not foster your love for your brothers and sisters in Christ the way that actually living with them will do. Love works and thrives by being in family. When you are in community, functioning as a family, you must choose to love each other on a daily basis despite how you may feel at times. Relationships are the seedbed for the spirit of family to grow in the church; you cannot have family without being in relationship with one another. Relationships create a safe place for people to feel valued, accepted, and loved. Ultimately, relationships call us to walk with God alongside one another. Living in community creates a place for this to happen.

After two years of being married to my beautiful wife, Holly, we moved into a community house of twenty-four people who were a part of Isla Vista Church. We moved into this eight-bedroom house, an ex-frat house, with our one-month-old, Samuel. Over the next two-and-a-half years, God proceeded to take me on a journey of discovering that church was never meant to be a place you go to, but rather a family you *belong* to. It was a journey of leaving my "I" mindset with my time, money, and resources, and entering a "we" mindset of sharing and investing in life together with others.

I had only been a believer for four years when God called me to the role of House Dad and Holly to the role of House Mom. The home was called *Shiloh*, situated in Isla Vista in between a frat house and a sorority house. The first year we lived at Shiloh the home consisted of two married couples, both in their first year of marriage, eight single guys, six single ladies, and us three. The second year, in addition to the twenty or so people living inside the house, two guys lived outside in an RV, one gal slept in her van in the driveway, and visitors often slept on the couches. Our daughter Hope was also born during the second year of living at Shiloh. In addition to all of this, the largest campus ministry at UCSB (Campus Crusade for Christ, known now as CRU) was meeting in a circus tent in our yard each week. Isla Vista Church also used the tent for our Friday night service before Jesus Burgers. Shiloh easily had hundreds of people coming and going each week and people dropping by quite frequently. Not to mention that as a community house, we shared not only living space but also our possessions.

Living at Shiloh taught me the meaning of holding "all things in common" (Acts 4:32). When we moved into Shiloh, the thought of making all of our possessions accessible was a bit alarming since we owned many relatively new gifts from our wedding registry. In life, I have found that our tendency to embrace an entitlement–approach is all too easy. I remember asking myself, "Am I really going to allow everyone to use all of our wedding gifts—from our super sweet kitchen dishes to our blender, knives, microwave, tools, and everything in-between?" The process of not hiding anything but making all things accessible was a heart battle that I had to work through with God. I believe that feeling entitled to our belongings is an American mindset rooted in many people. It was not until I moved into Shiloh that I discovered that this mindset of "mine" had a grip on me. However, over the next several months, as I began giving up these possessions and trusting God, I learned that nothing is truly our own. All we have, including people and possessions, is a gift from God.

I vividly remember one day God took me to Paul's rhetorical question to the church at Corinth in order to pry my hands free from all my possessions, "What do we have that we have not been given?" These words cut right to my heart, as I knew that I had been holding on to and protecting my possessions as if I earned and deserved them. God used this verse to liberate me and bring me into the greater reality of viewing all things as gifts to enjoy! That day he moved me from viewing my possessions from a "mine" men-tality to an "our" mentality. He continually gave me many opportunities to change this mindset.

I remember feeling that one of the hardest things to give up was my truck. I had a great solid-running truck, only three years old when we moved into Shiloh. It soon turned into the community house truck as people asked to borrow it all the time. Since we all lived in a college town, many people didn't own cars and often needed to borrow the truck to go to the store, haul something, or take a road trip. I didn't want to give up my truck at first, worried that people were not going to treat it with care. I came to later discover that my discernment was correct; however, I realized a person treating our things with care is not a prerequisite for lending out our belongings (oh, how I wish it was). The words of Jesus haunted me in the best way when people asked to borrow it: "Give to him who asks of you. Don't turn away from him who wants to borrow from you" (Matthew 5:42). It was as if I heard an audible recording of the voice of Jesus saying this verse each time someone would say, "J, can I borrow your truck?"

I believe one of the reasons why God calls His people to live in community is to break us of our individualistic mindsets, which cause us to be more concerned with ourselves than we are with others. Giving up everything to bless others became a joy that I wouldn't have discovered if I had continued protecting my belongings from people. Like always, in the two-and-a-half years of living in community, I discovered that Jesus was right when He unveiled the secret for finding life, "Whoever seeks to keep his life will lose it, and whoever loses his life will find it" (Luke 17:33).

What an upside-down way to experience the life we were created for with others. Giving possessions up causes the mind to become frantic with thinking, "What will I be left with if I give away my things?" The simple truth is that we already have the very thing we think our possessions are going to give us. The answer is God, and in Him comes complete safety, security, and fulfillment. Our vision becomes easily clouded when we have the wrong mindset toward the things that God has given us. They are meant to be gifts to be shared, not treasures to be hidden. When we participate in His Kingdom by giving generously, we begin to inherit the very life we thought the possessions would give us. We all know that safety, security, and fulfillment are never found in our possessions. However, like all kingdom concepts, we need to experience the truth to understand it. In the words of Jesus, "for not even when one has abundance does his life consist of his possessions (Luke 12:15)."

I have come to discover that this struggle with possessions, wanting to hide and acquire them for myself, was an outward reality reflecting an inward heartfelt attitude toward the community. We all have a tendency to hide from others at times, as I know I did before moving into community. I always tried to put my best foot forward, not wanting others to see my weakness and shortcomings in life.

Being a pastor and living amongst the people you are shepherding creates some interesting dynamics, to say the least. People catch on quickly that you don't "have it all together." I always said I was a man of many hats living at Shiloh. I never knew which hat would be needed before entering the door after coming home each day. It could be anything from husband, dad, pastor, friend, landlord, plumber, or mediator, to whatever else the situation called for. As I wore different hats, I discovered that God simply wanted to empower me to walk in love no matter the situation. Regardless of who it was or what they needed, He wanted me to love the person He was placing before me.

Especially during my first year living at Shiloh, I often struggled with loving people when I clearly saw their shortcomings day in and day out (as they undoubtedly saw mine). The enemy loved to put a magnifying glass on trivial matters such as blaming others for eating my food without permission, not paying rent on time, not doing dishes, or any number of other things. A big part of becoming a redemptive family is learning to love one another through our struggles. We need to be willing to fight to see our brothers and sisters in God's image, as He intended, even though there will be challenges in our day-to-day lives with them.

Before God called us to live in community, my tendency was to avoid getting too involved with people's lives unless I considered them friends. However, in community you can't always choose who to live with because God wants us to love all people, including those who may not love us that well or those who are not that easy to love. Jesus said it best in the Sermon on the Mount, "There is no reward for just loving those who love us." Living in community allows people to see and know the best and worst of each other. It's in this place of vulnerability and rawness that love is given permission to create a family.

Our high value on community living has become a core strength and reward of the Isla Vista Church family. All of our key leaders have lived in community with the family of God and have learned lessons through experience that only heaven can teach. In 2002 the Isla Vista Church family acquired a duplex home on the main street, Del Playa. It is the street infamously known for parties and is not drivable on Friday and Saturday nights due to the hundreds of people cruising up and down the street, hopping from house party to house party. This home is commonly known in Isla Vista as the "Jesus Burgers house" because its residents take part in a ministry that freely gives out hamburgers each weekend. The house consists of seven women on the top floor and seven men on the bottom floor. Living in this house is not for the faint of heart, as it undoubtedly requires your life. Every year I sign people up on the lease jokingly, yet somewhat seriously, by saying, "Sign your life away." I know for me and for many others, God used living in community to teach us the meaning of family through learning to share, contribute, and love one another with His love.

The stories you are about to read are from four individuals who have had their lives impacted in a significant way by living in community at the Jesus Burgers house. These stories testify to the journey of doing life together, sharing a home, and finding God's love for themselves and each other.

NO LONGER ALONE

DANIEL HAYRAPETIAN

Somewhere around sixth grade I noticed depression creeping into my life. Self-consciousness, timidity, and isolation cultivated a deep loneliness in me for the next several years. All of a sudden I didn't think that anything I did was worth celebrating, that people wanted me around, or that I was doing anything right. Overly critical and overly hard on myself, I spent my middle school and high school years wanting to be with friends but not being able to enjoy their company because I hated who I was. There was nothing cool about me. The best I could do was to be nice to people and make them smile. The only thing consistent in those years were the hours I spent alone and in my bed daydreaming about a life where I was cool and people hung on my every word. I tried to escape the thoughts that enslaved me and a pain that I couldn't get away from through heavy doses of video games, drugs, and sex, but nothing took away my loneliness for long.

On October 12, 2008, through a series of events that included getting put into a city holding cell for intoxicated people, I accepted Jesus into my life, and unknowingly, was invited to be a part of His family.

I would more clearly understand this truth when I moved into the Jesus Burgers house the following year. It was in this home that God walked me through a long season of coming out of loneliness and into family.

I entered the Jesus Burgers house with loneliness still hanging onto me. After I told my friends I followed Jesus, they started acting distant around me. Things weren't the same because I no longer wanted to joke crudely, smoke weed, or talk about girls all day long. And it had become so normal to feel this loneliness that I didn't think it was something I needed to talk to God about. I spent the year trying to befriend my housemates, but that loneliness still affected many of my interactions. At the end of the year, I understood God was good and wanted to set me free from my pain, so I wept on my knees, "God, please bring me great friends. And heal my heart."

God answered that prayer that following summer. Larry Daniels and I were going on a mission trip together during summer break. On the first night, everyone was assigned a roommate except for me. As the night got late, I wanted to hang out with my team and get to know them, but the all-too-familiar thoughts and feelings of depression, unworthiness, and fear of people haunted me and kept me trapped inside myself. *They don't want to hang out with me. I'm just lame. But I really want to go. No, I'm too lame. They won't like me.* The internal conflict raged until I heard a knock on my door. Startled, I opened the door and saw Larry. And with brimming gentleness he said, "Hey, bud, we're all hanging out down the hall. Come. We want you to hang out with us!" The thoughts stopped. The war came to a halt. I told him I'd be there in a minute. I closed the door and began to weep for joy. In Larry's few words I felt love, affirmation, and acceptance like I had never felt before. Nobody had said those words, "Come. We want you."

This relationship turned out to be very special, a Jonathan-and-David relationship. I echo David's words, "You were very dear to me. Your love for me was wonderful, more wonderful than that of women." Larry and I have spent hours listening to one another, praying for one another, and crying because the love of God hits our hearts so hard. God made Larry and me friends to fill up my heart with His love and free me from the loneliness I lived with for so long. I learned that God expresses His love and acceptance of me though His people, and it was okay.

A whole new perspective came into my life when I believed I belonged somewhere. God's family, He showed me, had to be an integral part of my life. It was what I was designed to live in and what I immediately became part of when I accepted Him as Savior. So, I spent the next year at the house with new freedom and life, pursuing deeper friendships and relationships with my family. The year was bountiful with breakthrough. But there was still one problem: I still felt that same isolating loneliness in the midst of God's great community, and I couldn't understand why. My journey was not over yet. He had to bring to the forefront a major wound that kept me from really living in family the way He designed it to be: I didn't like myself.

Growing up, I had always compared myself to other people. I wasn't fast enough, tall enough, good-looking enough, or confident enough. I believed that I was lacking something, and I needed to prove to others my value. God relentlessly told me that His love was all I needed, but that truth didn't hit my heart or bring much change for a while. When I was isolated from community, I just agreed with the negative and demonic thoughts in my head. And this resulted in me entering into relationships with people looking to get things from them. I would feed off of their love and affection, and when I didn't receive it, I withdrew into loneliness. I didn't know how to get out. But God had a plan. Learning to love myself was a task in which He used the whole family.

My third and final year at the Jesus Burgers house was revolutionary. God showed me that I was worth loving. My housemates' love for me was key as they persistently invited me to hang out, prayed for me, encouraged me, and fought for my destiny when I didn't believe I could achieve anything. This love became so penetrating that one night as I laid in bed and my thoughts screamed their familiar words of worthlessness, depression, and self-hatred, a new thought popped into my head that I'd never had in my life before, "I like myself." Simple, yet revolutionary. God broke me free. Through this freedom, I no longer hung onto people's affirmations or tried to gain their affections. Instead, I could enter into my relationships looking to give and not take. My relationships became healthier, and richer. I always came knowing I was valuable. I had something to give them, whether it was love, a hug, a smile, my time, or my listening ear.

By surrounding me with people who were so consistently amazing, God showed me that this was a picture of His love for me. He consistently likes me. He likes me even when I'm cranky, bitter, and selfish. He likes me for me. He didn't make a mistake when making me. It was in community that I realized God not only loves me, but He even *likes* me. I finally experienced God's love in truly liking myself. However, the story doesn't end here.

Today, the war still wages over my mind—to like myself, and to believe that God loves me and that I am worth loving. When I was working on writing this chapter, and struggling with what to write, I didn't like any of my ideas. Larry finally said, "Daniel, you don't like your ideas because you think other people won't like them. You think they aren't worth hearing. You're wrong. Go home, spend time with God, and when you know you're worth being heard, text me." It's in family that God gives me hope to hold onto, reminds me of what is true, and daily sets me free from loneliness.

This may all seem a bit blown out of proportion. You may say, "Just get up and get over it; don't be so shy, and have some self-respect. You're just thinking too much. Just live, love, laugh." But the things unseen are more real than the things that are seen. For those of us who grew up in broken families and never felt like we had a chance at feeling accepted, there are real and spiritual things that wage war over our minds, and only God can set us free from that oppression. I was lonely and God saw fit to set me in a family. And in this family, He's pouring His love on me and showing me that He wants every part of who I am to be a part of it. He allows me to be me, and to be loved.

BEYOND
SKIN DEEP

CASSIE AROYAN

I t was freshman year of high school when a new neighbor introduced Jesus to me. (Wow, thank you, Courtney!) She came into my life during a time when I desperately needed a rock to stand on. Even though my relationship with God lasted for merely a year, it was all the time I needed to know that He was there. My parents' separation happened from fourth to sixth grade, but watching them get back together only added to my confusion. Although I thought this reunion was miraculous, my younger sister and I witnessed it all fall apart again come the first week of my senior year in high school. Their marriage had finally ended in divorce, and my understanding of family dissolved with it. Then again, I'm not sure if I even knew what family was in the first place. Since I can remember, we hadn't eaten meals together, the homes we lived in were always big enough to separate us, and I rarely saw my parents express affection toward one another. It wasn't until recently that I discovered how deep the wounds of a broken home could be. This lack of covenant in my environment at home paved the way for my own un-committed relationships as I got older.

If there is one thing I can say, it is this: parents, love each other well. Your relationship is the most important miracle that your children are ever going to witness as such delicate bystanders. This is the best gift you could ever offer. I can't thank Jason and Holly enough for welcoming me into a real community as my spiritual parents and even friends. Their commitment to each other, their family, and IV church has demonstrated a covenant that I simply have not seen before. They are restoring my heart back to trusting in promise and simply belonging to a family.

God was preparing a family for me long before I even knew Him. He has since brought me into genuine relationships and taught me the value of community, despite the foundation my parents laid. However, throughout high school I was unashamed of my lack of respect for covenant. As the seasons changed, it was fairly easy for me to jump from best friend to best friend. The moment a relationship got rocky, I picked up and left, on to the next person without any shred of regret or guilt. Even though I carelessly flew through friendships, I always knew I could not survive alone; there has always been an incredibly deep, hidden desire for community within my heart. I quickly grew tired of playing the strong, individualistic girl who could take care of herself. But I continued in my ways, causing my desire for God and family to fade.

By the time high school ended, I was far too ready for the next chapter in my life. I desperately wanted to encounter new faces and new relationships. I moved seven hours away from home, leaving a three-year relationship with a guy and all of my friends except for one, Heather. I dove right into Isla Vista's darkness. I thrived off attention from men, confidence from alcohol, and petty connections with peers that I experienced through weed and various other drugs. Despite all of my idols, God remained faithful. He arranged new friendships with Christians who eventually invited me to Isla Vista Church. I saw a fire and a love for God within IVC that I hadn't seen anywhere else, but this alone didn't persuade me.

I continued down my path of destruction until summer arrived. I decided to go on a mission trip to Hawai'i because I had nothing else planned. I earnestly desired to love God, but the exchange of my current life of freedom for a life with God wasn't a fair trade in my mind. Nevertheless, it was in Hawai'i that I encountered the power of His presence. That single night is what caused me to completely surrender my heart and my life to Him; there was no turning back.

Summer ended, and sophomore year rolled around. I was fresh from a summer of soaking in God's love. I came back to Isla Vista a changed woman, and I was beginning to discover a new life of worth in Jesus. I was no longer partying and finding temporal satisfaction in the things of this world, so I moved next door to the Jesus Burgers house with fourteen other Christian students. That was an extraordinary year. It was the only recent year that the duplex next door to Jesus Burgers was filled with Christians. I was being molded for family. I was doing life with twenty-eight people who all radically loved Jesus. All the while we were living on the craziest party street in our city, Del Playa.

This was the year that God taught me the power of covenant in community living. Within the second month of being in my new home, I had a prophetic dream involving three friends and me. These friends consisted of Michelle, who I had known for one year, Heather, the friend from home I mentioned earlier, and Claire, who I had met only two months prior. The dream led us to the beginning of an eternal friendship that we didn't hesitate to jump right into.

One evening a visiting student from the International House of Prayer in Kansas City guided us through a prayer in which we committed our lives to one another for eternity. In the moment, this seemed like a wonderful idea, but in reality, we had no clue what we were getting ourselves into. Despite our immaturity, God knew exactly what He was doing with us.

The first few months of our newfound covenant was nothing but bliss. We consistently enjoyed one another's company as we started to get to know each other. Unsurprisingly, it did not take long for our relationships to get beneath the surface. We encountered boulders to traverse, rivers to cross, mountains to climb, and even a bear or two to fend off. This was the trigger in many previous relationships that made me want to run. The moment I entered a dark tunnel within a relationship, I wanted to find the fastest exit route possible. However, this usually meant leaving the tunnel alone instead of walking out of it with whomever I walked into it with. It was in one of these moments of tension that I meditated on the covenant we formed. I doubtfully asked God why we had even made that commitment in the first place, and it was in my unbelief that God gave me incredible insight into the meaning of relationships. In the gentlest way, He said,

I let each of you enter this relationship in your immaturity, because it meant that none of you could exit when these hard times came. Cassie, you are so used to running away. You've run from every relationship that got hard because your lack of commitment made it easy to leave. By saying yes to these girls for eternity, you are being forced to look for the light at the end of the tunnel. Without covenant, family, and deep, intentional relationships, when times got tough you never had the hope

to search for the light. But that's because you
never even searched for the hope. Now, since
you know this is for life, you're forced to look
for that light and to have hope through these
rocky times.

This hit me hard; it was all true. I never needed
to look for the hope while enduring tough times because I knew I could run. My relationships had always
been shallow enough to easily leave them behind, but
there is nothing shallow about God or anything that
He made. Praise God that through finding the light
and hope within our eternal commitment to each
other, we were able to get through these tough times.

I no longer desire to walk away from relation-
ships. God has given me the grace to persevere when
I encounter tunnels in my friendships. In covenant,
God can get me through anything.

After my revelation with God, as an alternative of
letting impatience and frustration cloud my friendships, He taught me how to react in love for others instead of wanting to remove myself. I no longer focus
on how someone hurt me; rather, I ask myself, "What
is in my heart that is making me react with these emotions?" This made all the difference. Instead of building bitterness in my heart toward a friend, I work
to grasp the root within *me* so I can dig it up. This
means not trying to fix *them*. This allows me to approach friendships with humility, understanding, and
wisdom, an approach that has turned out to be vital.

This group of friends and I also had to quickly
learn that the best cure for any situation was going
to God first. Covenant allows for a safe place to be
vulnerable, so there have been countless times that
we have prayed together. Even when we were resis-
tant, these prayer sessions always turned out to be so
amazing because God always showed up. Choosing
to be in the light about situations is something we

learned the hard way; all the same, this is what has saved us. We also learned how to walk alongside each other through each of our trials. When I go through a hard time or isolate myself, I now take a step forward instead of taking a step backward. This is where humility, understanding, and wisdom fashioned a way for me to be completely there for my friends and them to be there for me in times of need.

No longer is there a selfish way out of my relationships. God is eternal, love is eternal, I am eternal, and the relationships with the people I love are for eternity. I am no longer a slave to circumstance. We are designed for community, each and every one of us. And while most of us come from broken homes, having developed fears of being known beyond our surface, community is simply what we were designed for. Community needs to be the new normal. Isolation is not and never should be normal.

I am currently in the second year of living in the Jesus Burgers house and this church is now my family. Since being with this community, I've discovered a dream within me of creating a collective farm where this family can do life together. We can raise our children together, interact on a daily basis, and share everything. No longer will the fences of the American spirit and dream isolate each family; we belong together! It is by the grace of God that I even have this dream, but it only testifies that I now truly value community and believe in the significance of family.

I've been challenged, pushed, and pulled. I've broken down and have so desperately wanted to run, but my family doesn't let me because they love me. They are for me and believe in me. When we claim to be Christian, not only are we saying yes to Jesus, but also we are saying yes to every part of who He is, including His family.

Everyone is welcome. There are no prerequisites,

and I can promise you that there is no secret password at the door. There isn't even a door if we're doing church in the Lomelinos' backyard, the Book of Acts style. Isla Vista has been waiting for a revelation like this for a while—a revelation on the power of family, the power of adoption, and the true power of love. Our city is designed for community; all of the students are within walking distance of each other and barely anyone lives alone. All the while, IV church is eating meals together, we are genuinely caring for one another, and we are simply just doing life together. We're not being tamed. We're purely being changed by love as we learn how to trust God and embrace the constant glory of community.

LET THE WALLS COME DOWN

CLAIRE ANDERSON

In spring 2012, I found myself standing at the front of Isla Vista Church as part of the "good-bye Sunday" tradition in which I was supposed to tell everyone my plans post-graduation and then receive prayer. I was completely overwhelmed as I looked out into the crowd. The tears were uncontrollable as I made eye contact with all the faces in the room. Two years prior to that moment, I did not know a single one of these people I now called my family. Jesus used that community to do radical things in my heart that have shaped who I am, how I live, and how I view God. I moved directly into the Jesus Burgers house from the dorms the summer after my freshman year at UCSB. Initially, I came in as a sub-leaser, not knowing that I would call it my home for the next couple of years. At that point I had never been to Isla Vista Church, had not met Jason, and did not know anyone in the house. A series of divine encounters with people and God led me to commit to the house that summer, as He had recently challenged me to begin actually acting like the Christian I claimed to be. It was the biggest step of faith I had ever made on my own, and in retrospect, I can confidently label it as the step that changed everything for me.

My walk with God began as a child with ten years on the mission field of Eastern Europe with my parents and four siblings. Then in 2001, to my horror, we moved to a suburb of Los Angeles to start a church. The transition was rough, and struggling to learn dollars and Fahrenheit, I quickly realized none of my new friends would be able to completely relate to me. Not to say that I didn't have fun, make friends, or enjoy my middle school and high school years; however, my friendships lacked depth. It was easier to joke around and avoid the subject of elementary school or my parents' occupations. It is not an exaggeration to say that maybe one or two of my closest friends even knew I had lived overseas. I developed a fear of being misunderstood. I was confident and happy, and I did not see the value of letting other people into my heart.

The idea of vulnerability made me cringe. In an effort to protect myself, I built impenetrable walls around my heart. Needless to say, an adjustment was necessary when I moved into the Jesus Burgers house and began attending IVC, a church whose focus on family and community is unprecedented—straight from the Book of Acts. In one respect, my previous mindset helped provide intimacy with Jesus because I knew He always understood every aspect of my heart and life, but the way I had closed off my heart to others did not leave much room for beneficial relationships, spiritual growth, or evangelism. Frankly, I did not see the importance of any of those things.

For me, the greatest challenge of the Jesus Burgers house was not that of living with fourteen other people and the inconveniences that come with living in a ministry home, but rather being around legitimate Christians all the time. It was a challenge because this made me realize that I had tailored Christianity to include only the things that I liked and felt comfortable with. But these people I now called housemates were not the cheesy or fake Christians I had expected. They were intentional with me—shallowness was not an option. They asked questions with genuine care. Within the first couple months, each of them knew me better than anyone I had previously labeled my best friend. It is important to note that it had nothing to do with magically compatible personalities. In fact, we often joke that if it weren't for God, none of us would be friends at all. The love available through community is completely dependent on Jesus. The love that we receive from Him enables us to love others, and our relationship with Him allows us to understand the way He sees and values people.

Living in community inherently pushes us into greater depths with the Lord. I was introduced to and quickly inducted into a church family in which I was given freedom. This freedom allowed me to dance, to dream, to sing, to prophesy, to question, and most importantly, to fail. During my first year in the house, I remember my three closest friends, Cassie, Michelle, and Heather, praying for me to receive the gift of tongues. We prayed for this gift a couple of times on different occasions. They were eager for me to experience God in a new way, but when I didn't receive it initially, to my surprise, it wasn't awkward or weird. We just proclaimed God's goodness and sovereignty over my life. We would go out and pray for people to be healed, but if they weren't, we still left the situation encouraged. I learned that even beyond spiritual things, just in doing life together, that when we fail we need to be surrounded by people who encourage and love us in the same unconditional manner that Jesus does. This unconditional love continues to push us into our destiny regardless of the daily circumstances.

Living in the house made it impossible to become

stagnant with God. My community loves me enough that it pushes me to ask God for more, to step out in the prophetic, to pray for dreams (literal and figurative), to ask to hear Him more clearly, and to love people as Christ loves us. As humans, we are designed to be in relationship—with God and others. We need to live in transparency and vulnerability, encouraging each other on a daily basis and establishing deep friendships. This is the essence of church family; we need this type of community so that when times get hard (and they will), you have support, acceptance, and safety. For me, the times got hard right at the end of my time in Isla Vista. In the prayer shed one Friday night with Jesus Burgers in full swing outside, I found myself bawling as God tore down all the walls I had spent years building around my heart. With graduation two weeks away, I had started moving out since my graduate program and new job had already begun in Los Angeles. In the midst of packing and good-byes, one of my best friends opened up the topic of dating, although he was about to move 2,500 miles away. It seemed as though everything was happening in the worst timing ever, and I finally had to admit that I could no longer tough it out, muster up a smile, and say everything was okay. Jason joked that God knew exactly what crazy circumstances it would take to get me to a point of admitting my need for community, and He wouldn't let me leave IV until that happened. Jason was completely correct. Before that night, while I had enjoyed community, I hadn't yet understood the real importance of it. In that moment of weakness, as I went through the most transition I had ever experienced, I was in a prayer shed behind a house filled with the most loving people I had ever encountered. I was sitting on a sofa next to my pastor and spiritual father who had chosen to invest his life in college students like me. I was surrounded by people who had spent the past two years caring for me, listening to me, and praying for me. I was overwhelmed with thankfulness for this family; it was about time I realized that I needed these people in my life. I finally understood that vulnerability is not synonymous with weakness and that it is okay to admit you need help. God is very purposeful with whom He places in your life, whether or not you are aware of it. To have your heart fully exposed is a scary way to live, but Christianity without Christ-like community is unbiblical. In the same way that God Himself has relationship within the Trinity, He has created us to live in relationship with each other. No matter how great you think your relationship with God is, it can only get better when you honestly open yourself up to other people in the safety of the church family. God does not want us to waste time living in fear of being misunderstood or not accepted by man.

I now know that the walls around my heart were unnecessary and foolish. The Lord wants to protect our hearts for us in order that we can trust people and fully delve into the community we so desperately need.

REDEEMING FAMILY

LINA SHIN

I remember when I was a young child and my family was still a family. I have faint memories of nights out bowling and family walks around the neighborhood, sweet memories that seem almost unreal now. When I was in fifth grade, my parents split up and everything changed. My dad left and my mom began to spend long hours working late to provide for my three siblings and me. I longed for love and affection, but it was nowhere to be found. I learned from a young age to build walls around my heart to protect myself and never trust anyone, because everyone let me down. I remember nights in high school feeling lonely and lost and wanting so badly for God to show up. All I wanted was for someone to love me and care for me, but I was left feeling lost and abandoned. God is good and showed up in the most unexpected ways, teaching me once again the meaning of love and family.

I grew up going to church every Sunday and attending a small private Christian school from third to twelfth grade. I said the Sinner's Prayer in third grade at a chapel and spent most of my youth going through the motions of being a "good Christian," but never really knowing God. Although I was immersed in Christianity, it was all just a bunch of head knowledge. I didn't understand the concept of an authentic relationship with God; all I knew were rules to follow. Little did I know that everything would change in a small college town known as Isla Vista, infamous for its wild parties and loose lifestyles.

I came to UCSB as a wide-eyed freshman, completely unsure of what exactly I had gotten myself into. Prior to coming, any time I mentioned the fact that I would be attending UCSB I would get the same sly smile and look of surprise since everyone knew UCSB as one of the biggest party schools in the country. I, on the other hand, was always the goody-two-shoes who never partied, drank, or got involved in that scene. Here I was entering UCSB, a school known for its infamous parties. But God in His graciousness met me even in the darkest of places. I immediately got plugged in with a Christian group on campus and began to meet people who were authentically in love with God. It was through this campus ministry that I learned about Isla Vista Church.

They were known as the radical Christians. I wasn't exactly sure what that meant, but I had heard enough about them that I wanted to experience IVC for myself. I began attending the church during my sophomore year. From the beginning I understood what people meant by radical, as they worshipped freely and loved extravagantly; I fell in love. During that season of the church, we were meeting in Pastor Jason's backyard, also known as the Sueno Tabernacle (they live on Sueno Road, and a canopy had been erected for meetings). I have so many fond memories of encountering the love of God in that backyard and in that home. My first year with the church was filled with learning about who God is and actually understanding what it means to live *with* God not just *for* God. I began to hear the voice of God for myself and to see the ways He was intricately involved in every detail of my life. I learned about the Father heart of God and the extravagant love that He has for me. All of my brokenness, loneliness, and pain that were hidden deep inside of me from my youth began to resurface. For the first time, I chose to face it instead of hide. The love of God covered every surface of my heart and brought healing like nothing else can.

As I began to commit to Isla Vista Church, I realized that I wasn't committing to merely a church—I was becoming a part of a family. Fears of rejection, abandonment, and a lost concept of family had to be broken and rebuilt in safety and love. A lot of that learning happened during my time of living in the DP house, also known as the Jesus Burgers house, which is located on Del Playa, the biggest party street in Isla Vista. Thousands of college students walk up and down Del Playa looking for the next party, the next high, the next hook up. We sit in the middle of it all, offering a simple burger and a lot of love.

I lived in the house during my senior year. Our house was filled with a variety of personalities, each of us unique in our own way. We all had different approaches to eating, studying, sleeping, and cleaning; and we were really only united by our love for Jesus. Sometimes all of that uniqueness created tension. Some of the girls didn't eat like I did, didn't wash their dishes like I did, didn't do this or that like I did, and the list would go on. It was easy for me to resent those differences and become frustrated, but thankfully, it wasn't long before God came and revealed Himself in the midst of it. Living in the DP house wasn't just about living with people, it was about creating an intentional community where we were always for one another, choosing to love each other extravagantly.

Each of our unique personalities remained the same, but pursuing God together made loving each other easier. Instead of only seeing things my way, I began seeing things God's way and my heart changed. Washing extra dishes became a joy knowing it would bless my fellow housemates, and letting go of differences to serve my sisters proved to be rewarding. I began to enjoy the times when I cleaned—whether we all cleaned together or I cleaned by myself—because cleaning was an act of love rather than an obligation.

Choosing to love created a safe atmosphere in our home. Some of the sweetest moments in the house were when someone would come home completely broken, exhausted, and beaten down by what the world had thrown at her. She didn't have to hide it when she came home because she was safe to be exactly how she felt, knowing that we were there to love her and pray with her. When we had our worst days, coming home meant there were six girls ready to pray, six girls ready to listen, six girls ready to affirm God's truths, and six girls ready to love. Coming together in the midst of our brokenness led us into deep humility, seeking God's face and leaning on one another as a family.

We really were one another's family, and we loved each other through all the moments. Whether it was sharing a meal or having an intense game night where yelling and competitive personalities raged, there was always love. Love is what kept us close and set our house apart from all the rest. On some nights our house was like any other, a bunch of college students hanging out and doing silly things. But what made it different was our genuine love and care for one another. We learned to love each other even when it was difficult and to have hard conversations even when we didn't want to. This lifestyle taught us that there really is no fear in love, and love always wins. In one short year, this family proved to me that we could love each other when we disagree, and though it isn't always easy, it is definitely worth it. This sincere love for each other poured out into the city. Compassion fueled us to freely open our home every Friday night to a city of lost and broken college students and welcome them in with open arms and open hearts.

Living in the home freed me and taught me to dream big for myself. I remember one night last May, sitting in the house of prayer (our converted garage) and hearing God tell me that I was going to Honduras. I had no idea what that meant or what it would look like, but here I am now, a few months later, sitting in Roatan, a bay island off of Honduras, writing about the family that propelled me here. Even thousands of miles away, I still feel connected and loved by that family. Just this morning one of my former roommates from the DP house sent me a message with words of encouragement from God, just because. Because that's what family does. We love extravagantly, not through our own strength and might, but through God's love. God in His goodness brought me together with a group of mismatched people in a small college town and taught me what family is all about, and I'll never be the same.

UNIQUELY MADE, DIVINELY PURPOSED

DERRIN SCHULTZ

I was raised in the church from birth. I grew up attending Sunday school, learning stories from scripture, and singing worship songs. At age five I told my mother that I wanted a relationship with God, and I gave my life to Jesus. Around ten, I told my mother I wanted to be baptized, explaining to her that I understood it was a public declaration to God, the world, and myself that I belong to the One who created me, who knows every hair on my head. But, even in spite of this, I didn't truly understand what it meant to be a Christian and live a life consecrated unto Him. In high school, I began to notice inconsistencies in my relationship with God. At this time, Holy Spirit began to highlight examples of my interactions with people, and how my behavior differed at church, home, or school. This unsettled me, so I chose to be one person—either the Derrin I was at church and home or the Derrin I was at my high school. Not just to act the part, but to truly decide which Derrin was worth it—which one would be life giving—not only for myself but also for those around me. I already knew the answer. But it had to be real; I couldn't just pretend. I had to choose to change things—change my friends and change what I was exposing my heart and mind to.

One of the ways this change manifested was in removing myself from the group of "friends" I spent time with at my high school's bus loop every morning before school. The majority of these kids had already, by fourteen years old, experienced drugs, alcohol, and sex. I had not. So why was I hanging out with them? Granted my time spent with them was not during the partaking of these vices, but during the graphic retelling of such events, and the crude jokes associated with them. It was shortly after the initial nudging of God's Spirit telling me, "Derrin, this is not good for your heart" that I submitted my verbal resignation to these peers whose lives looked way different than I knew mine was supposed to. I plainly and respectfully told them that I wasn't going to be hanging out anymore. I let them know that I cared for all of them, but that I didn't agree with or practice the same things as they did, so it was time to move on.

This obedience to God's Spirit, and my willingness to potentially endure ridicule and loneliness led to a deeper hunger for the things of God. This hunger was not satiated by the hour-long Sunday service at my church's high school group. I had graduated in my spiritual diet from milk to meat.

At this time, which was still my freshman year in high school, I began going to a Friday night college ministry called Reality, which met at Calvary Chapel Santa Barbara. It was here, around 2002 or 2003, that some people shared testimonies about their ministry on Friday nights out in Isla Vista, Santa Barbara's crazy, local college town, which I then despised and where I now reside—go figure. During this petition for prayer warriors and those with a heart to love the lost, the birth of a ministry house was also announced. This house was to be smack-dab in the center of Del

Playa, Isla Vista's main party street. In those early years the darkness was thick and the warfare was intense; believers would literally shake with fear and become nauseous to the point of vomiting as they approached the enemy's playground. But the blood of the Lamb goes before His children and sweeps over the land like a river of purifying fire. Aslan is on the move in Isla Vista; the increase of His Kingdom shall not diminish nor end.

So, what does any of this have to do with my life or community living? Well, during my senior year of high school, when I was looking for a place to live following graduation, my mom suggested to me, "What about that Christian house in Isla Vista?"
"Live in a house full of complete strangers in that God-forsaken city? NO WAY!" I thought. But God, in His ever-gentle way said, "Remember how interested and excited you got about that house when you first heard about it a few years ago?" So that settled it. I began meeting with the leader of the DP/Jesus Burgers house after school once a week to discuss life and the possibility of living there the following year. I eventually moved into the DP house on Friday, July 7, 2006. I had no idea what I was getting myself into, but it turned out better than I could have ever imagined.

If there is one thing I have learned from God through community living, it's that your life and the choices you make affect not only you, but everyone you live in community with as well. If you expect to live life in community assuming no one will be affected by foolish, impulsive, and prideful choices, then you're reading the wrong book and serving the wrong god.

I learned this in a real way during my first couple of weeks living at the DP house. At the time I was in a relationship with a girl who was also raised in the church and professed to be a Christian. However, our relationship was not one that honored God or submitted to His leading, rather it was one driven by our own desire for each other.

In my second week in the DP house the Lord reminded me of the story of Achan in the book of Joshua. This man had taken plunder from a conquered city for himself after the Lord had specifically told the Israelites not to. Because of this one man's sin, the entire nation of Israel was negatively affected. At the next battle against a tiny nation named Ai, the Israelites were defeated, even though they far outnumbered their enemy. They lost the battle they should have won because the Lord departed from them as a result of Achan's hidden sin. The Lord said to Joshua,

> Israel has sinned; they have violated my covenant, which I commanded them to keep. They have taken some of the devoted things; they have stolen, they have lied, they have put them with their own possessions. That is why the Israelites cannot stand against their enemies; they turn their backs and run because they have been made liable to destruction. I will not be with you anymore unless you destroy whatever among you is devoted to destruction (Joshua 7:11-12 NIV).

These verses haunted me, and the Lord very plainly asked me, "So Derrin, Me or her?" as if to ask me, Who are you living for? Who is Lord of your life? Who will never leave you nor forsake you? Who can give you real fulfillment and purpose? I knew what I needed to do if I wanted to fully experience the purposes God had for me as well as the brothers I was living with. I didn't want my hidden sin to hinder the amazing things God had in store for my house as a whole. Thus, I broke up with my girlfriend at the end of my third week in the DP house.

God's Word says, "And whether one member suffer, all the members suffer with it; or one member be honored, all the members rejoice with it" (1 Corinthians 12:26 KJV). This verse comes to life in community living. Even in the smallest things you can tell whether brothers and sisters are suffering or rejoicing. You can tell by the way they steward their time, studies, and chores. The music they listen to, the movies they watch, what they talk about, and how they respond to certain things or people reflects the state of their heart.

This is why as members of the body of Christ we should encourage one another to be who God intended us to be. We should intercede on behalf of whom we know our brothers and sisters truly are rather than what they are acting like. It was in my fourth year of community living that God gave me this revelation: other parts of the body can't fully appreciate, understand, or encourage me if I am not embracing who I was created to be. The other parts of the body also cannot fully operate in their calling unless I am truly living out mine. "And the eye cannot say to the hand, 'I have no need of you'; or again the head to the feet, 'I have no need of you'" (1 Corinthians 12:21 NASB).

The fact is, we all need each other. All people have specific gifts and revelations that only they can impart to the other members of the body. How boring would it be if God's body were all feet and no hands or all eyes and no ears? The body of Christ needs a brain that can instruct the feet to walk forward on the path of life so that the hands can pick up and feel what the eyes are seeing. You were uniquely made and divinely purposed—believe it. Though you may not receive any praise from man or share the spotlight among your peers, God's purposes are fulfilled and His Kingdom advances as you live like the son or daughter He made you to be. Rejoice in the knowledge that only you can be you, and as you abide in that truth, others are released to walk in that same freedom.

Community living has definitely blessed my life beyond anything I could have ever imagined or asked for. It has challenged me to love people through their insecurities, unhealthy habits, and dark pasts in order to see who they were made to be. I can honestly say that it is all worth it. We will not always perfectly carry out the things God calls us to or perfectly love the people He has placed in our lives, but He is all knowing and all loving, and He is working all things together for the good of those who love and serve Him.

There is more going on beneath the surface of our hearts than what we can see or ever hope to see. At times we may feel like such a small part in the lives of others and that our efforts aren't even making a difference. But in this we can be certain, God is faithful to weave together the time, love, and prayers we share with others into a beautiful community.

Conclusion

Lucas Bell

Living in community with other believers is the most tangible way to experience life together as family. Although it is not a prerequisite to be in a spiritual family, it does provide ample opportunity to live life together on a daily basis. The closeness experienced in this time will build relationships that are as close if not closer than our blood family. We are provided with opportunities to share our lives and our possessions. We are given the freedom to contribute to God's work in each other's lives, pouring out His love on each other.

While community brings out everything in people, it also draws us into each other's hearts. As we see each other's strengths and weaknesses, and they see ours, we learn to value each other through unconditional love. In the proximity of sharing living space, we see each other at our best and our worst. In the hard times, we run toward issues not away from them, because we are aware God is maturing us. Issues will not get resolved unless they are confronted in honor for one another. Community living is not perfect, but God matures us as we handle the situations. His faithfulness continually manifests as we chose to love each other with His love. In the safety of community living, we draw close to one another, and we truly begin to value each other. The practice of honor and value is fundamental for family.

In the mindset of living intentionally with each other, we discover the beauty of family and the restoration of relationships. For most, community living forces us to deal with the pains of past relationships that we still hold on to. As our lives are exposed to other people, we must chose to embrace this vulnerability and go deeper with each other. Because we have one another in our lives, God will use others to bring us to a greater place of understanding of His love and commitment to us. As we learn to receive God's love for ourselves, we are empowered to love others. Community puts us in the perfect position to receive from each other. Our spirit comes alive as those around us take the time and energy to nurture us. In this exchange of life, we realize our need for each other and that God really does not intend for us to live our lives alone.

Living in community forces you to love people, not just talk about loving them. It is the most practical guide to living out the Kingdom at all times. Community living is a place for unconditional love and irresistible grace. In living together, we will find our differences, but we must always find our common bond in the Person of Jesus. Our mutual love for Him will propel us deeper into His heart for more of Him and each other.

In the journey of community, we are constantly faced with opportunities to get out of the "I" mindset and into the "we" mindset. When we live with other people, we cannot just think about ourselves or view our possessions as our own. Through sharing our lives together, we have the privilege of sharing everything that God has given us. It is then our delight to continually devote our lives to one another, giving freely of our possessions and our time.

Community living gives love the permission to create a family. In this process, we will share meals, struggles, messes, possessions, prayers, and dreams with each other. Through rawness and vulnerability, we are challenged to love each other no matter the circumstance. These situations keep our hearts soft before God and tender toward one another. When grace is revealed in family, we cannot help but love each other more and more. Brothers and sisters become family in community living as they learn to share, contribute, and love one another.

Daniel needed community to teach him that he was no longer alone but rather made for family. Through living in community, God freed him from self-consciousness, timidity, and isolation. Through family, he realized that he did not like himself. However, God taught Daniel to love himself through his housemates loving him well. In doing life together with other people, he was allowed to be himself and be loved at the same time. God's love released his heart to love himself and be an active member of a thriving Spirit-filled home. Community living opposes every thought of independence. In turn, it frees us from isolation and loneliness. In family, we discover that we are no longer alone, but a part of an everlasting love.

Community taught Cassie the meaning of family. When her parents divorced, her understanding of family dissolved. Through living with other believing women, God reconciled and healed her wounds. Community not only taught her about family, but it also fulfilled her longing for healthy, committed relationships. She traded her independence and loneliness for a family full of faith, hope, and love. Here, God rebuilt her understanding of relationships through the power of covenant. Her covenant with three friends placed her in eternal relationships, which her fear of commitment could not destroy. As we live in community, God teaches us to approach our relationships with humility, understanding, and wisdom. The presence of these creates a safe place to be vulnerable with each other. Community living imparts to us a sense of eternity, as we understand that we are loved by covenantal family.

It was not until two years of living in community that Claire finally recognized the importance of community. Moreover, she realized that it is okay to admit that she needed help. Living as family requires a transparency of heart and the willingness to be vulnerable with your life, thoughts, and feelings. It takes a heart willing to receive from others in order to live in freedom with other people. Claire opened her heart toward covenantal relationships. In community, she was around genuine Christians all the time, forcing her to redefine her walk with God. She experienced the love of God through the people she lived with, pushing her into greater depths with the Lord. God uses community living to keep our relationship flowing with Him. As our community loves us, we are given the freedom to mature with God and step out into our gifting and dreams. Living with family provides us with around-the-clock encouragement and edification, no matter the situation. As we open ourselves up to other people, we will experience more of God. When we pursue life together, we spend our time trusting one another as God takes us deeper into our redeemed lives.

Lina spent the later part of her childhood and teenage years building walls around her heart, feeling lost and abandoned. She desperately wanted someone to love her and care for her. It was not until she came to IVC that God began to reveal Himself to her through a community that worshipped freely and loved extravagantly. As family led her to the Father heart of God, her brokenness, hurt, loneliness, and pain were replaced by the love of God. This compelling love drew her into family, causing her to belong not just commit to a church body. This family provided her with the opportunity to live in community with others. Here, she learned to overcome both differences and living-style preferences in order to create an intentional community. God revealed Himself in the midst of her living situation, empowering each of her housemates to love each other extravagantly. As she lived with other believers, her heart changed to love her roommates in their individuality. She began to see things God's way; He provoked her to choose love and live this out daily. This love created a safe atmosphere in the girls' home. These girls became family as they learned to love each other day after day. In this home, Lina saw family redeemed and love become real. The experience of community living will not only set us free from past wounds, it will change our entire lives, as we love each other with the Father's love.

Community will teach us that we are made for one another. Somehow, in the grand scheme of God's great plan, He places us together for His divine purpose. Even though we may not always understand this from the beginning, we must embrace each other as God's own. In the process of living together, we discover that our actions and lives are more interwoven than we may realize. For community to flourish, each individual member must be healthy and whole.

Derrin left his peers because he knew they were not seeking after the things of God. His hunger for God empowered him to risk ridicule and loneliness, leave his current circumstances, and seek intentional community. He soon learned that his life was not his own in community. His life was drastically affecting all those around him. With a desire to preserve integrity and wholeness, he left his girlfriend in order to pursue the amazing things God had for him in community.

Living together is a direct look into each other's lives; you can tell the condition of their hearts by the state of their lifestyles. We all need each other to live a life that is whole in God; when one suffers, we all suffer. We must be willing to both rejoice and suffer with each other. We need each other to develop who God made us to be. In this place of commitment and freedom, God's Kingdom advances as He weaves us together as a beautiful community.

The love of God continues to show up in the midst of community living. Mismatched people become family, eternal relationships are formed, loneliness is defeated, restoration occurs, and the testimonies of transformed lives continue to increase. God is breaking the spirits of independence, isolation, and loneliness through intentional community. God formed community living in order to give us fellowship with one another, which grants us the completion of joy. Intentional community overflows with the joy and love of God. Devotion to one another overcomes the challenges that arise. The Spirit of the living God comes to rest in a community that is intentional in its relationship with Him and each other. Our mindset toward doing life together through community living brings love to life as we, "bear up under everything and anything that comes" (1 Corinthians 13:7).

2

Fathering and Mothering

"For if you were to have countless tutors in Christ,
yet you would not have many fathers, for in Christ
Jesus I became your father through the gospel."

—1 Corinthians 4:15 (ESV)

Fathering and Mothering

Holly Lomelino

Parenting children is a hard task no matter what. And yet we live in a time and culture where the challenges facing those who are raising children are even more paramount than perhaps ever before. Broken families are the norm now, and few adults have had godly examples to look to in their attempt to grow up. Maturity is not something that is guaranteed with age, and having an orphan heart is possible for even those with two living parents.

We live in a day and age where most parents are too busy or too inexperienced to know what it means to truly mother or father a child. And many of them were not properly loved, cared for, and trained up by caring, nurturing parents themselves. It is very difficult to be a good parent without first experiencing good parenting as a child and being genuinely cared for and led in the ways of the Lord.

God has taken Jason and I on quite an adventure of first teaching us to be His children, then helping us grow in maturity, and then teaching us how to become parents. It is a process that has a natural rhythm and order to it. As we learned how to be loved, nurtured, and taught, we naturally wanted to grow and give that away to others.

As parents to four young children in the natural,

which has been a wild and crazy ride to say the least, learning how to parent grown college students in the spiritual has been equally an adventure.

There was a season at IVC when we were actually criticized for not having mothers and fathers. People were concerned that we were just a bunch of young people with very few older people to give us wisdom and direction. It wasn't that we didn't want mothers and fathers in the faith to join us; it was that they didn't want to come. Isla Vista and our church were a bit too much of a stretch for most people from the older generation.

But God was simply telling us to "dwell in the land and cultivate faithfulness." So we did. And before we knew it, we *became* the mothers and fathers. Though still young, we learned faithfulness and that our Heavenly Father had fathered us. He grew us in wisdom and maturity through the trials and tribulations He walked us through. Then He started bringing us children. Just like in the natural, God doesn't wait for us to be perfect and totally mature before He allows us to be parents. He gives you the children and then grows you in the process.

I think in a lot of ways it snuck up on us. For me, it began with God calling us to adopt Annalisa Morris, at a point in which I still barely knew her. Of course, you don't get to pick and choose your natural children and don't really *know* them before you give birth, so I guess in some ways this was the same sort of thing. We just received her and trusted in God's voice as He called us to do this. We obeyed without asking too many questions. Just like having a new baby born into the family, you aren't too sure what all to expect. You just receive that baby and hold onto God's hand and let Him lead you.

That's what we did with Annalisa. Fortunately,

she didn't come with too much physical responsibility (God knew I couldn't handle another child to feed, change, and bathe), but the spiritual and emotional needs were very real. She needed someone to care for her and listen to her, someone to guide her and offer her wisdom and discipline, and someone to rebuke and encourage her. She had a solid faith and a huge heart but was never nurtured by a spiritual family that could grow her into the godly woman she was made to be.

Around this time, God was calling Jason and I to surrender to Him the number of natural children we would have. He asked us to trust Him—trust Him with how many He wanted to give us and when He would bring them. We said yes, and only later realized this was going to apply to our spiritual children as well.

"Behold, children are a gift of the Lord " (Psalm 127:3). We choose to agree with Him on this; we said, "We will take as many children as You want to give us." And so they kept coming. Lindsay was already Annalisa's sister in the faith, and how can you adopt one child and leave behind her sibling? Next came Krissy, a more broken child who needed a little extra love and care. Then the next thing we knew, Jason and I were becoming parents to many of the students, to varying degrees. It became apparent that they were almost all in need of a mom and dad, people they could come to for wisdom, advice, direction, and encouragement.

Along with all this loving encouragement, there was also a need for teaching, loving rebukes, and accountability. We knew it wasn't going to accomplish much to set up a class and lecture them about faith and life. It needed to be in the context of real life and relationships because what one person needed was sometimes the exact opposite of what the next needed. And for the most part, they didn't need more teaching. They needed love and care. They needed someone to listen to them and encourage them in their faith. They needed safe places to be real and vulnerable and share the reality of their struggles and dreams. They needed someone to speak into their lives from a kingdom perspective and help them gain new perspectives on themselves and life. So God gave them a mother and a father. And it was only our availability and willingness to receive them as gifts from God that qualified us.

Jason and I would be the first to admit we have no idea what we are doing most of the time. But that's okay because their true Father does, and He is the One we are leaning on in this journey. He gives us the wisdom, for He is the One who had the plan in the first place. It has felt much more like we are simply stepping into this kingdom truth of mothering and fathering that He is laying out before us, than us creating some great idea of how to do ministry.

While I have so much more to learn as a parent, and will never really know everything I wish I could about how to be a good parent, there is a lot God has shown me over these last eight years of motherhood. One important thing I've had to learn is how to really teach and train my children. There is a saying that goes "more is caught than taught," and this is particularly true for parenting. I can tell my children all day to speak calmly and kindly, but they will only learn that if I am living it out. If I am yelling at them and hysterical all day, you better believe they will follow in my example. It is a startling thing when you first hear your two-year-old say something exactly how you have said it, whether it is good or bad.

I think this reality of parenting is precisely why Paul encouraged believers to find fathers in the faith and not just teachers. Someone can tell us how to live all day long, but it is when we see it modeled before us that we are somehow empowered to live it out. Having open homes and open lives is such an important part of becoming mothers and fathers. It has been people's access to Jason and I that allows them to feel like they have spiritual parents, people they can experience the mess of life with. It is being able to see Jason and I have a tiff and then apologize or to watch us lose our family van with no plan B and continue to trust Jesus that equips our "children" to live a life of faith.

One of the greatest lessons I've learned in parenting, especially with our grown "children," is inheritance. It is the concept of freely giving our children all that we have worked and labored for, without requiring them to do the same. All that we have learned in the Lord, all that we have had to fight and contend for, they get to simply walk into. And while we as their parents have had to sacrifice for that, it is such a joy and blessing to see others step into maturity so much easier as a result of our labors. Our ceiling has become their floor.

Even my own parents have given me an inheritance in this way. They both grew up in broken homes that lacked consistent, healthy family experiences. When they met and got married, one of their high commitments was to have their family life be much healthier than either of them had grown up with. They had to fight hard for this, and it wasn't easy. While far from perfect (as no family is), they were able to create a family for my brother and I that had love, communication, and commitment. We ate dinner together as often as possible, went on trips together, and enjoyed many activities together. My parents were very committed to being involved in our lives and equipping us for life. They fought to give us a better family life than they had growing up, and I am extremely grateful for that. My own children are now the beneficiaries of the inheritance my parents gave me. Now it is easier for me to grow and develop the revelation of family in my own home. My mom says that I am a much better mom than she was in many ways. Sometimes I don't know how true that is, but to the extent that I am, it is because of the inheritance she gave me in mothering.

One example of this concept with our spiritual children has been in hearing the voice of the Lord. There was a season in my life when I spent hours in a prayer chapel at Westmont College learning how to quiet my mind and listen to God. It took a lot of time and discipline, and I had to fight for it in many ways. But I am so thankful for those times because I learned to hear His voice, one of the most precious gifts on earth. So, of course, I want to teach this to my children and see them walk in this same reality.

I remember when I began teaching Annalisa and Lindsay about hearing God's voice. They were hungry, and I was committed to seeing them experience hearing Him in their own lives. They began to engage in the discipline of meditating with the Lord and quieting their own voice to hear His. I was so joyful as they began to hear from Him so clearly themselves. I soon found myself going to them for a word from the Lord! It was exciting and humbling to see them be able to step into this much more quickly and easily than I had. I began to experience one of the greatest realities of mothering both in the spirit and in the natural. So much of what it means to mother or father another is to lay one's life down for them. It is to sacrifice your own rights, desires, wishes, and glory so that others may go far beyond what you ever could have dreamed.

Another incredibly significant part of parenting is obviously discipline. Jesus called us to go and make disciples. Coming from the same root word, it follows that discipline and discipleship go hand in hand. God truly desires that we all would have people in our lives that we give authority to speak into our lives, not only for encouragement but for accountability and discipline as well. He desires for us to be submitted to one another, not so we would be hindered but for our protection.

> Obey your leaders and submit to them, for they keep watch over your souls as those who will give an account. Let them do this with joy and not with grief, for this would be unprofitable for you (Hebrews 13:17).

We have a biological daughter who has really struggled to rest in her identity as a child. She wants to rule the world and is incredibly independent and strong-willed. It is very hard for her to submit to us as her authority, and it often causes both dangerous and unpleasant situations for the both of us. Watching her fight so hard against the blessing God wants to give her in resting in our authority, I have learned so much about God's heart to teach us how to submit our lives to others. He truly desires to spare us much grief by allowing us to learn from other's wisdom and insight. One of our spiritual children also had this same struggle, and at one point she wanted to go on a mission trip for the wrong reasons and against our counsel. While we of course allowed her to go and supported her despite her dismissal of our thoughts, it was painful to watch how big of a mess this decision caused for her walk with God. But as loving parents it was not our job to control her, but rather to share the insight God was giving us and walk with her through the mess her choices made. Discipline is necessary in all parenting, but in any situation we must remember that God's mercy triumphs over judgment.

God has also taught us a lot about parenting with grace. This means we understand that our children are unconditionally loved and accepted independent of what they do, and that we are never going to give up on them. It has also to do with not micromanaging their lives, but instead teaching them how to hear God's voice and discover the blessing found in obedience to Him. We encourage them when they mess up and forgive them when they make poor choices. Having grace means offering wisdom and counsel when need be, and even a timely rebuke when God makes it clear to do so.

Parenting with grace means nurturing and caring for hearts in a world that often wants to knock us down and beat us up. We all need someone to believe in us and push us toward our destiny, someone to tell us that we are going to be okay because God is doing a good work. Spiritual mothering and fathering has a lot to do with these things. It is seeing things from a higher perspective and helping bring the younger ones in the faith up to that place. Essentially, nurturing their faith.

Above everything else, I think the single most important aspect of spiritual parenting is learning how to do it by faith, led by the Holy Spirit. This means getting God's heart for the people He calls you to commit to and then loving them with the Father heart of God. It means listening to what He is saying about who they are, what He has for them, and what He is doing in them and teaching to them right now. Then, it means coming alongside the Holy Spirit to be God in the flesh for them. Helping people tangibly experience the heart of God has been the most powerful part of being a spiritual mother. Some days God calls me to hug one of my spiritual daughters for a ridiculous amount of time to break her outer shell of independence and rejection, while the next day He asks me to sit a spiritual son down for a firm but loving rebuke about some issue in his life. Just like with children in the natural, the needs vary from moment to moment, so we must learn to keep in step with the Spirit.

God knew that in order to have a family, mothers and fathers in the faith would be needed. It is definitely an adventure to embark on this journey, and it is not for the faint of heart. Nevertheless, committing to relationships with other believers and becoming a spiritual child or parent to someone bears much fruit and is incredibly rewarding. The more we experience these types of real and devoted relationships with one another, the more the Kingdom of God will take root and grow on the earth in a powerful, unstoppable way.

THEY
RUINED ME

ANNALISA MORRIS

There's a common joke among the counseling psychologists that all your problems
lead back to the two people who brought
you into this world: your parents. "They ruined my
life, Doc." That's not all there is to it, of course. Sure,
they have a profound influence on us, but we all impact each other; no other person can be at fault for all
your problems.

My parents loved me imperfectly and from their
own brokenness, yet they loved me a whole lot—and
that's more than anyone could ask for. I grew up not
knowing anything besides divorce. My parents split
up when I was about two, so I thought that it was normal to have two houses, two beds, and two separate
families. The family I saw in old home videos wasn't
the one I knew. It wasn't until much later in life that
I realized I had a few things missing from the social,
relational, and emotional equation. My parents did
the best they knew how with the broken pieces, and
I have to say that I turned out okay. God is faithful to
fill any lack I have.

But just as parents have the chance to ruin you,
they also have the ability to shape you. They can give
you the grace to make mistakes and can show you the

way to succeed and dream. I've been blessed with not only great, loving biological parents but with great, loving spiritual parents too. That's just the kind of God I have; He loves to give me the double portion.

I came to Christ at the ripe age of eleven and decided to follow Him with my life. My parents supported me in my decision, but they definitely did not always understand my relationship with God. I grew in Christ and religiously followed the dos and don'ts that I thought would lead to eternal life. Little did I know that eternal life was to know God, not just follow Him.

I went away to college in a little party town called Isla Vista, still trying to do the right thing and finding little life in it. I discovered the Jesus Burgers ministry, and my life slowly got turned upside down. When I found out that the God of the universe not only knew me but also liked me, things quickly changed.

I met Jason at Jesus Burgers and felt really comfortable and safe with him. At the first prayer meeting I ever went to, Jason prophetically gave me a verse that to this day is a promise over my life. It meant so much to see people who cared about me and saw God's heart for me even when they barely knew my name. I kept hanging around because strange and glorious things happened when I did. I was hungry for more; these people kept feeding me, so I kept coming.

One night in May, I rode my bike across Isla Vista to go to the Lomelinos' house. I pulled up to the house ready to encounter whatever God had for me that night. We gathered around the small laptop screen, watching the Lakeland revival in Florida being streamed live on GodTV. It was all new to me, but something inside me came alive when I witnessed prophecy, healing, and other acts of the Spirit. After the web stream ended, Jason put on worship music.

People began to pray for each other and encounter this same God we had just witnessed on the tiny screen. I sat on the couch and relaxed next to Holly. Jason passed by us with a smirk and a glimmer in his eye that I've come to know so well. This look can only mean that the Holy Spirit is up to something. Jason came back and knelt before me with a bowl of water and a washcloth. Before I knew it, he removed my worn-in Rainbow sandals and began to wash my feet. Tears sprung to my eyes, as they are apt to do, a reflex Jason was quite used to at this still-early point in our relationship. He began to pray and prophesy over me, speaking of the way I was a servant and a blessing. Jason exchanged a quick glance with Holly, wanting to confer with her but having no opportunity to, then said with full confidence that he felt like God was calling them to spiritually adopt me. Holly shrugged and smiled, supporting her husband in his spontaneous plan. I had no idea what it meant at the time, and they didn't really either, but it began the most fruitful, life-giving relationship I've known to date.

I was stunned that Holly and Jason would commit themselves to me and my dreams without even knowing me. They had a faith in God like nothing I had seen before, and they were choosing to pursue covenantal relationship with me simply because He said so. Jason took on a fatherly role, always wishing to guide and protect me but never afraid to push me beyond my comfort zone. Holly was quick to nurture and care for me while also sharpening me with her honesty and wisdom.

I began to hang out with their family more and to see what it was like to genuinely live life with them. I think I've learned more about God from watching Jason interact with his daughter Hope than any workbook or sermon could ever teach me. I learned from Jason and Holly what covenantal love looked like where no example served before. They showed me through their disagreements and imperfections that they were still committed and always for each other, no matter what. It was strange to see that such a love really existed. It wasn't a fairy tale, and it didn't always seem like rainbows and butterflies, but there was true love there that was never giving up and never backing down.

I started to see them push me into my destiny and stretch me in ways I did not expect. They were always there for me, but not always there to make things easy for me. I began to hear the voice of God and to seek His ways for everything from my college major to my weekend plans. Life had its ups and downs, but I felt grounded and supported by Jason and Holly through it all. One thing I gained from them was confidence in myself and in my relationship with God. Whenever I came to them for advice or attention, Jason and Holly's first words were constantly, "Did you pray about it? What did God tell you?" When I would sheepishly reply that I hadn't really prayed about it yet, they were quick to point out that that was my real problem. If I wanted to lean on them, they knew that I really needed to depend on God first and foremost, so they always redirected me His way.

I think my temptation is often to try to be God for other people, especially those who need me or who look up to me, but that is not a lasting solution. It was Jason and Holly's job to point me to the One who could really meet my needs and satisfy the longings of my heart, not uselessly try to fill them themselves. They were always careful to let me know their opinion and challenge me to figure out the answer on my own as well. These aren't people looking to find more followers or clones. The true calling of fathers and mothers is to help their children shape their own way and find themselves in the process.

Jason and Holly are not perfect. They have failed me at times, and I'm sure they will again. But they are quick to own up to their mistakes and to force me to deal with the fact that failure and mess are part of relationship and do not equal the end of relationship — something I had not encountered before. My life is no longer defined by the value I feel in my relationships. I've learned that love is a commitment and that the way God feels about me cannot and will not be changed. I've found myself, and I've found that I have nothing left to lose. If they could take a risk to love me, though they fail, though I fail, then why couldn't I take that same risk for others?

Their love and encouragement gave me the strength and courage to go after my dreams and overcome my fears of imperfection. I've been privileged to mother a few girls in our church as well; I've committed to love them through the good and the bad. I am pioneering a prayer house in this college town, and I don't think I would be doing it if it wasn't for the support and encouragement of Holly and Jason. That's the thing about covenantal love: when it's safe and it's for real, it can give you the foundation to build upon, the backbone to stand, and the wings to soar.

This all really hit home when I got to witness them renew their vows after ten years of marriage. Flowers had been placed all around, guests came dressed in their best, Holly appeared in her wedding gown, and Jason stood with tears in his eyes. Here were the two closest people to me showing me what commitment and love really look like. They've shown me time and time again that I'm worth that same sacrifice, and that nothing will change that. My eyes were opened to the beauty in love that is long-suffering, the safety in knowing you'll never be abandoned, and the perfection that is provided by Christ's sacrifice. Then the tears came, and I felt assured that through the good and the bad, these things will never change: the love of a father and mother and my inclination to cry at almost anything.

So, I guess I come to the same conclusion that we started with: they really did ruin me, but in the best possible way.

MADE FOR GREATNESS

KRISSY MASON

I was made for greatness. I believe that now. Now, I *really* know that with everything inside of me. It seems the enemy tried all my life to make sure I never knew that.

I want to first say that my parents are amazing; the courage it has taken them to get from surviving to thriving in this life will always serve as an inspiration for me. I only hope I can carry such courage on to my children. I'd also like to say it's not their fault. It's not their fault that their firstborn (my sister) died suddenly in a car crash and they didn't know how to cope. Like so many of us, we carry our wounds from a broken family into our adult years. As a child I didn't have the compassion or grace growing in my heart to see that they, too, were simply children of God longing to stumble across help or healing. God showed me that my parents are His kids too, and this helped me release them from my grip of resentment and bitterness. I can truly say that my mother and father did what they could in a time when tragedy exposed all of their weaknesses.

I was thirteen when my sister died. I can't say that the death itself was where all the pain came from, but it's for sure when it started. When Ashley died

I didn't just lose a sister, I lost a family. It's hard to remember anything prior to that event. However, I know there was a time when laughter filled my house, long summers were packed with mom's adventures, and evenings were spent scurrying away from dad before he tackled his girls with tickles. There was a time when we all watched movies and ate popcorn on Friday nights, a time when we all sat together around the dinner table. I pray to God that He helps me recall those pre-tragedy memories, for they became so distant and vague after her death. In their place I felt a pain I'd never known before, a horrible mixture of hatred, bitterness, and lingering depression I couldn't shake for over six years. It was like a flood of hell entered in, and the enemy used our pain as ammunition against one another.

After she died my family disappeared; each one of us found our own dark hole and sat there attacked by shame, guilt, and fear. We were each haunted in our own way. I desperately needed a family, but the family I knew was lost in the tragedy of her death, never to be found in the same way again. I was thirteen and alone.

Shortly after her death, my parents divorced and my mom began dating. I felt abandoned. Back and forth between two houses every other week wasn't what got me. It was the fact that each house would have my mom or dad in it, but neither of them was really there. I felt like I exhausted them; I was either too much or not enough. I wanted to please them so badly, but when I couldn't I despised them.

From this set in an identity based on lies, which took years for God to break me from. My identity was this: I am not worth the investment; I need to get out of the way of people because I always cause them pain; I need to do things on my own because no one will take care of me. I locked up that truth in my life and accepted my new cold and hard demeanor, thinking it was a brilliant coping maneuver.

I wished it were me that died instead. I thought Ashley got the easy way out. They held on to her too tightly, and I was so mad at her. I wanted my parents back. I wanted them to forget about her death and remember me.

I became very out of control, and I learned to manipulate and lie, to cheat others and myself. I used manipulative ways to get attention from my parents and other people, ways that hurt others and myself and only resulted in the wrong kind of attention, filled with misdirected anger from her death. I had so much rebellion inside of me. I remember being driven by hate. The worst of it was that I couldn't cry. I was so hard and mad and didn't want to lose face or my power. I figured out the power of being hard and numb, and I wasn't ready to lose it easily. I became the lies that I believed. The perpetual cycle of feeling undesirable grew as my heart turned to stone.

In an attempt to get away from it all, I found God in Santa Barbara, California. I got truly saved, and that magical moment led me to a relationship not only with Jesus but also with Holly and Jason Lomelino. They are not old enough to be my parents, but they sure have a revelation on how to mother and father a wounded and wild heart like mine. I was in complete shock by their love. The first words Jason ever said to me were that God wanted me to rest and be a daughter. I sure had never felt like a daughter, not God's or anyone else's, and I certainly didn't know how to rest. It was profound that God knew exactly what I needed. Jason felt that God was calling him and his wife, Holly, to adopt me as their spiritual daughter. Only time would tell what a gift it was that they obeyed the Holy Spirit. Their loving commitment was the most tangible example of Christ's love and commitment to me.

Before I met them I was at a big, busy church distracted by my immature desire to become "something" in ministry. I was hurt and shocked that God was calling me out of that place. Reluctantly, I listened to God and stepped away from that church and into His arms, truly for the first time. Holly and Jason took me in; I was scared to be loved and pursued and never thought I was worth the kind of attention they offered me. God didn't want me in a church building working *for* Him; He wanted me in a family working *with* Him.

Holly and Jason opened their lives to me by inviting me to family outings at the farmer's market or to sleep on their couch. For the first time, I had a safe place to cry, mourn, yell, hate, and eventually love. They listened, and they invested. It wasn't counseling; it was an exchange of lives. Together we became something greater. We became everything of what He fought for us to be. We became a relationship, a *real* covenantal relationship that was unconditional. I received more from this relationship than being preached to at a service could ever give me.

As their unrelenting love pursued me according to their faith, questions and worries plagued my mind: What do they want from me? I can't give them anything. What's in it for them? I hope I don't do something wrong because I am beginning to really like them.

I thought there had to be a condition that went with their commitment. Believe me, I pulled all the stops to test their commitment. I yelled and complained and attempted several times to resent them and run away. I didn't understand why they loved me so well, and in a way, it made me mad. Don't they know what I have done? How bad of a person I have been? Why are they taking my power away by getting me to feel so safe and vulnerable? It drove me nuts at first, but they never moved from a place of consistent, unconditional love. It was always a "come as you are even when it's ugly or messy" mentality. Their love drove my old identity away by combating the spirit that told me I was undesirable. They made me feel wanted even in the midst of my pain and sin. I was still desired, still fought for, still pursued, and still valued.

Their love was unchanging despite my behavior. Isn't that the gospel? I mean that's the Jesus I know and love today. If you are reading this and don't know that it's a "come as you are" and not "as you should be" gospel, you have been following the wrong gospel. He died while we were YET sinners! It was a powerful thing when these two people displayed that reality to me; it brought me closer to the Jesus I had been waiting for my whole life.

Walking through this process with Holly and Jason, I feared I would eventually become too much for them and they would give up and leave. I would think, "Oh this time I have really done it, really screwed up." But they never left. They never changed. They were always for me. They walked me through past hurts; they walked me so far past them that when I wanted to use my old pain for an excuse, they wouldn't let me take pity on myself. They refused to let me forget about the victory that Jesus has won and that I was not ruled by my past anymore. They always pushed me forward, forward into the destiny Christ always had for me.

I am boasting about these two, but I am really boasting about Christ in them. Not once did I ever get the chance to idolize them. They never let me. Their responses always pointed me to Jesus and how to steward His voice and His thoughts for my life. I felt so empowered to have a relationship with the Godhead on my own, not relying on them as a crutch. God became very real to me, and the flood-gates opened. Through real intimacy, Jesus replaced my heart of stone with a heart of flesh.

One memory that will always stick with me was Holly's mandated "hug" time. It had become very apparent to Holly and Jason that I hated touch and intimacy. It was too much for me; I was still a little too skilled at keeping people at a distance, even though plenty of walls had already been penetrated. For a season Holly felt called to break me of not wanting to be touched. During these months our discipleship time didn't consist of lengthy conversations or Bible discussions; it consisted of the simpler, but much more challenging, physical touch of love. I had to come to their house most days and stand there and let Holly hug me.

I can't tell you how hard this was at the time. Until I met the Lomelinos, I ran. I ran away from everything and everyone. Her holding me so tightly and intimately was the scariest thing in the world. For years I didn't let anyone get close to my heart, and it was like she was inside of it, knowing me more than ever. It was my last shred of independence and hardness disappearing, and she hugged it away. I would stand there crying and trying to wiggle away saying, "Okay, I am fine. This was great; now we are done." But minutes would go by, and we were still in the middle of the room, her holding me, and me weeping. As my spiritual mother, she was physically loving me into a greater place, so I would have the capacity to love others well from a soft, healed heart.

It's been over four years since my orphaned little heart met my spiritual parents. I am whole and have joy, and it's because they saw hope in Jesus transforming me through them. They had hope for my life and for God in me.

Our relationship has evolved: Jason performed

my wedding ceremony and in many ways has become more like a brother to my husband and me. While Holly and I have become more like best friends than mother and daughter, our love is still rooted in a covenantal and unconditional love. Now years later, Erik (my husband) and I look forward to mothering and fathering people into the greatness God always had in store for them. It just takes someone to say yes to relationship, yes to investment, and yes to sacrifice.

INTIMACY IS RICH

LINDSAY SLAVIK

O n the first day of my first season of swim team, I had a pool party for my fifth birthday . . . perfect! Inner tubes and noodles were everywhere, except near me. As I searched for my inner tube in the deep end, I grew tired and my strokes got weaker. I started to panic when I saw my mom chatting away with the other moms, completely distracted. "Why does the kick board seem so far away," I thought, as my heartbeat became louder and faster. In less than seconds, my mom saw me and dove in the pool head first, fully clothed, to my rescue. Smiling with love in her eyes, she picked me up in the water. I was a little shocked and embarrassed that *my mom* dove in like that, and that I even needed her to save me.

Almost two decades later, and now I am a sophomore and a dance major at UCSB; God brings me back to that memory, one I thought was long gone. Holly, my *spiritual* mom, comes into her kitchen with bags of vegetables overflowing out of her arms, two of her children running around, and her baby crying in her hands—a pretty chaotic scene as she preps to feed about fifty people at our church/family gathering. I am standing at the table ready to help her cook when her gentle eyes smile at me. She asks me how I'm doing. I tell her, "good," even though I feel far from it; but I know we don't really have time or privacy to talk further, so I decide not to go on. She continues to stare at me, looking deeper past my "good," so I start stuttering out bits of what is really hurting my heart. Meanwhile people are coming in and out of the tiny kitchen, getting ready for worship, the kids are all calling to Holly, and the baby is still crying. But Holly doesn't seem to be phased by any of it; she drops her bags, drops her agenda, and embraces me. She hugs me and begins to pray for me as tears fall from my eyes. I feel so loved, so safe; I barely speak and she knows what I need; she knows me. As she holds me, that pool-party memory flashes into my mind out of nowhere. Holly is diving in head first, but this time it is for my heart.

Rewind again, back to my childhood. It was seriously the best. I grew up in an incredible family. My mother and father loved me and believed in me. Encouraging me to run after my dreams, my parents instilled in me the belief that I could do anything. There was healthy discipline in our home; a common line from my folks was, "even though I'm upset, I still love you just the same, and I always will." I knew they meant it. No matter how badly I messed up, they would never stop loving me; I was safe and free to grow, knowing failure was never the end. However, outside the home was where love and safety were counterfeited and scarce. As I entered into my teenage years, lies of body image, competition of talents, and reputation among social circles left me wounded and broken, confused about who I really was and what my dreams really were. Those chaotic, teenage years passed in a blur, and I found myself in college away from that scene but still engrained with lies.

Relationship was the device God used to break

the patterns of lies and wounds in my life, patterns I didn't know were there, patterns I thought were normal. I grew up knowing God was real. His truth was written in my heart, but I put up so many walls to protect me from the pains of this world that *I* didn't even know my own heart anymore. But God had a plan to use spiritual parents and a lot of tears to break down those walls.

I met Jason Lomelino on a Friday night at Jesus Burgers in one of America's craziest college towns, Isla Vista. He was introduced to me as the pastor of Isla Vista Church, the church that created Jesus Burgers to serve drunk college kids and simply love them as Jesus does. Jason was not a man of many words, and at first glance he seemed way too young to be a pastor, so I never thought our relationship would go beyond acquaintances. But to my surprise, it did. I was later invited to a barbecue at Jason's house where I met his wife, Holly, who is equally ordinary. Holly was calm and seemed emotionless, with eyes that appeared to be bored and disapproving of me. She totally hates me, I thought. Even her smile and welcoming words were nonchalant and unconvincing. We were so different in so many ways, and I thought I would never hang out with them after this barbecue. But somehow I felt something deep and special between us, a connection beyond anything we knew at the time.

To be honest, the whole relationship was very organic in how it formed. After a few months I found myself frequenting the Lomelinos' house to ponder dream interpretations, babysit their kids, deliver groceries, or hang out—just living life together. We saw each other at our best times and worst times, but it didn't matter because our relationship was founded on more than circumstances—it was founded on God. And God is about covenantal relationships that are unbreakable and safe; He's about family. Family is what Jason and Holly became to me as they adopted me as their spiritual daughter. It was like I began life all over again, but this time as a daughter of God in the Lomelino household.

Even though the pool parties and teenage struggles became faded memories, I still was consumed with earning my status, whether that be through a high GPA, dance achievements, or a good reputation. Striving for excellence controlled me, and coming to college to have a "free will" did not change anything. In the midst of this, I met God, who led me to the Lomelinos, and the Lomelinos led me back to God. But they brought me to His throne room and showed me intimate relationship with Him, something I never knew was possible. Just as my real mom dove for me in the pool, Holly pursued me, invested time in me, and came to know me as a daughter. In this season of my life she knew what I needed to get through the deep end.

The summer before my junior year of college, I lived at the Lomelinos' house for a couple weeks in between housing changes. At this point we had been building our relationship for a year and a half, though it had felt like a lifetime. That summer I took four classes, though most people cringe at taking any more than two classes. But I was determined, or crazy. One afternoon I came home exhausted as usual and found Holly on the couch nursing her baby, Jeremiah. I collapsed on the opposite couch wanting to cry with exhaustion when Holly looked at me with stern eyes and said, "Lindsay, you do too much. You need to learn how to rest. Have you asked God if you should be doing all of these classes?" I just stared for a few seconds, shocked that she said that and expecting her to be more sympathetic. "What? No, Holls, I didn't ask Him. I just need to take these classes to graduate . . . What do you mean rest?"

"Lindsay . . . ," Holly began to preach, "God created the heavens and the earth in six days, and on the seventh day He rested. He created a day of rest for a reason, so that we would rest from our work and trust Him with our lives. He wants us to come before Him and connect one-on-one, not once a week, but every day—to meet with Him first, and let Him lead our days. God did not create us to strive and get so overwhelmed with our schedules that we don't have time for relationships, especially with Him. You need to get alone with God and wait on Him, ask Him what He wants for your life, and wait for Him to speak to you." So I did.

I went to the beach with my towel and journal to wait for God, and He came. His voice was subtle but clear as He told me to discontinue nearly all the activities in my schedule and solely pursue the dancers in the UCSB Dance Department with His love. Rest was never a tangible or purposeful thing for me, so I was bewildered to hear God lead me to this simple calling.

From then on, God began to grow my heart for the dancers as I trained, rehearsed, and shared life with them everyday. He helped me choreograph beautiful stories of His grace and love and highlight whom I should pick for my cast. Over the next two years, almost a dozen of the dancers encountered God, and five of them surrendered their lives to Him. God specifically appointed two of the girls to be my spiritual daughters, one of which happened to be in my choreographed piece. It was in those rehearsals that God began to open her eyes to the truth, and soon my spiritual daughters were hearing God's voice, prophesying, and leading other dancers to the Lord. Today the legacy continues: a handful of the saved dancers are bringing God's glory to the department and choreographing dances inspired by heaven. It was insane, and it all happened because I rested, waited to hear the Lord, and obeyed His plans for my life. And that is His will: to know Him and to be known by Him.

The culture of family that Jason and Holly established allowed me to hear God's voice, learn to rest as a lifestyle, and lead others into His glory. Their ceiling became my floor, and my ceiling became the dancers' floor as each victory we gained allowed the next generation to experience God with greater ease. Holly took me under her wing and showed me how to fly. She was my guide to the throne room, where true intimacy and rest with God is found. If it weren't for that season of rest I would have failed to recognize all of the times God was speaking to me, and missed out on His magnificent plan of revealing Christ to the dancers at UCSB. I am forever changed; free from striving, free to be myself, free to live out my calling, and free to teach others the same. I am able to soar from glory to glory with God and help others to fly all because of Holly and Jason's pursuit and intentional commitment to me.

Mothering and fathering younger lovers of Jesus is about believing in who God created them to be and enabling them to walk in His specific plan for their lives, from glory to glory! That comes from investing time in them and encouraging them in their lives. That's His will, and my story is a testimony of the fruit that Jason and Holly have been producing in their home. There is no system for how to do this. God is so creative in how He speaks, how He loves, and how He fathers. We get to do the same for others, so they can experience a relationship with their Heavenly Father, too. Intimacy is rich; it's to know and to be known. It's Jesus.

HE CALLS
ME SON

BRIAN PARK

My story with Jesus unfolded on the basketball courts during the summer of
2009. On a nice summer day, my friend
David and I decided to go play basketball at a local
park. Ever since I met David, he consistently asked
me to go to his church, and every time I refused. My
persistence met its match that day when David boldly
stated that if he made a three-point shot I would have
to go to his church at least once before the end of
summer. Just for laughs, I agreed. With a big grin on
his face, he took the shot and made it. Astonished, I
argued that if I made the same shot I would not have
to go. I took position, aimed, and shot. As my hand
released the ball, I slowly watched the ball scratch the
rim and fall to the ground—I am convinced that the
only reason I missed was because an angel came and
blew it off course. Forced to keep my end of the deal,
I bitterly agreed on going to church.

On my way to church, I eased my nerves with the
possibility of befriending new people. Surprisingly, I
enjoyed my first visit and I decided it would be harm-
less to continue attending on a weekly basis. Months
rolled by, and I slowly became accustomed to the
church and was inevitably confronted with the "would

you like to accept Jesus as your personal Savior and Lord?" question during one Sunday. Concluding his sermon, the pastor announced that if anyone wanted to receive Jesus they should come and talk to him. With my hands sweating and body trembling, I approached the pastor and timidly discussed becoming a Christian with him. After that, I considered myself a Christian, but in reality, I was far from one. My paradigm of Christianity produced a Pharisee-like, religious zombie rather than a faithful son consummated by divine romance. My lack of an intimate knowledge of the Person of Jesus Christ caused me to forsake Him and give popularity, friends, and a girl complete possession of my heart by senior year of high school. My heart yielded to the fading pleasures of drinking, partying, and sensuality.

In the midst of my spiritual enslavement to the carnal nature, there was still a small remnant of me hidden deep down that screamed for freedom. God heard my cry, and though I didn't recognize it, He began to resurrect in me a new creation. By the end of my first semester I broke up with my girlfriend, and with a renewed mind, I saw the things I once enjoyed for what they truly were: foolish vanity. Jesus continued to violently fan the flames of love in my heart, and by the time second semester started, I witnessed Christ in me intensely manifest His presence and His ownership of my heart. I began co-leading a campus ministry called POP21 (Power of Prayer in the 21st century) and I co-founded another campus ministry, At the Gates, which met at the front gates of the four high schools in our district to pray for revival in our respective schools. In the meantime, He took me into a season of unimpeded spiritual growth, moving from glory to glory. Though I was initially unaware of the prophetic ministry, the Holy Spirit radically encountered me during the International House of Prayer's

(IHOP-KC) Onething regional conference and baptized me in the Spirit. Then, He began cultivating my prophetic gifting by having me attend a local college ministry that actively walked in the prophetic. Next, God led me to do a three-week internship at IHOP-KC called the Luke18 Project where He more rigorously grew and pruned me. But He was far from finished.

During my last night at IHOP-KC, through a mutual friend, I met Heather—attendee of Isla Vista Church and now my neighbor—who at that time was doing a different internship. Upon learning that I was going to be an incoming freshman at UCSB, she told me about Isla Vista Church, the Isla Vista House of Prayer, and a ministry they have called Jesus Burgers where people experience God in gnarly ways. Although I was getting amped from hearing all of her testimonies, I did not think of IVC as anything more than a church for me to attend. Little did I know that IVC would become to me so much more than just a church!

In fall 2011, I moved to UCSB and immediately went to check out IVC that Sunday. During service, people were laughing, jumping, dancing, and experiencing the Holy Spirit. It was here, standing before the pews ecstatically admiring everything before me, that one epic chapter of my life came to a close and the next chapter began—a chapter I will hold closest to my heart.

Before I go any further, I must give a brief synopsis of my childhood. My mom worked in South Korea and was able to visit our family only twice a year. The distance itself speaks of my lack of closeness with her. My dad excessively worked as well, and he also had a disposition to drink. To me, he portrayed exactly the kind of man I aspired never to become. They worked tirelessly to have the best for my family, but their illusive fabrication of the "American Dream" consumed them. Paying the bills and saving money to buy a house took preeminence over actively participating in my life, and I adapted by living an independent life by the time I entered middle school. As my heart grew more numb and callous toward my parents over the years, my ability and desire to communicate, relate, and love them faded.

Coming into Isla Vista Church, I was amazed and overcome with jealousy of how intimately acquainted everyone was with each other. What I saw was unrecognizable, almost bizarre, to me. What I saw was a family bonded by unadulterated friendship that had no other agenda than to selflessly love Jesus and others. Jason often tells us that because the family is so close and familiar with each other, it is almost intimidating for an outsider to come into the church. That was my experience during the first couple months in IVC. Although I attended church, went to every weekly meeting, and even became Facebook friends with a lot people, I still treaded along the peripheral of this family. All of them related with each other in a way that I did not and could not. My heart longed to be able to fellowship with them just as they did with each other.

Then in May 2012, IVC held a retreat. I eagerly signed up, hoping that the retreat would be a great opportunity for people to know me more and for me to finally achieve that relational status everyone maintained with each other. Though during our first day of the retreat I ate meals with them, engaged with them in group activities, and dominated them in a game of Mafia, I still remained relationally distant. By the end of our first night I recognized the all too familiar sense of loneliness and separation. I dismally acknowledged the erected Jericho walls in my heart that kept me at an arm's length from enjoying the glorious bliss of friendship and family found in IVC.

To close our last night, we gathered to corporately worship and encounter the presence of God. As people flocked into the living room, I sat there hoping that God would encounter me in a way that would assure everything was going to be okay. Mac began to lead worship, and things were quite normal for the first couple minutes. It was not until about thirty minutes in that Jason took his one-year-old daughter, Joanna Joy, and sat her on the back of my neck, put his hand on my head, and prophetically declared something to the group. By now, I had come to understand that some unusual things can happen in any prophetic ministry, so I did not think much of it. However unusual it may have been, this prophetic act was a physical manifestation of God's promise for me. Nehemiah 8:10 reads, "The joy of the Lord is your strength," a verse He has proved to be prophetically significant in my life time and time again. A couple minutes later, Jason took Joanna off of me and held me in his arms. I simply broke down weeping because it was as if Daddy Himself was holding me in His arms with my head resting against His chest and His banner of love hovering over me. Holly soon came over to comfort me, and Jason spoke the Father's heart into me. Of all the things he said, what I remember most clearly is, "Brian, we receive you."

It was that proclamation of adoption into family that brought down the walls in my heart. I could not help but continue to weep as I experienced the Father's love tangibly overwhelm me through Jason and Holly. That night was not only a turning point in my life with IVC but also a time of intensive healing and irresistible freedom. Jesus came and picked me up from the ashes of my past, crowned me with Sonship, and clothed me with brothers, sisters, a mom, and a dad. Truth be told, I had a mother and a father growing up, but I lacked a mom and a dad.

I came to Isla Vista Church as an independent child with a fragile identity stained by loneliness. Now I am part of a family, still a child but now being nurtured by the care and love of the most amazing spiritual parents. I share many similar characteristics and passions with Holly, which makes it enjoyable for me to talk and relate with her. She is a mom who provides safety, encouragement, and comfort. Jason gently and patiently labors to see Christ formed in me, strengthening me to walk on my own two feet. He is a dad who portrays just the kind of man I hope to become. I found the fulfillment of all my childhood familial longings in my spiritual family at IVC.

The morning after the worship, I woke up early to help with breakfast. As I walked toward the kitchen and greeted Holly, she said to me, "I was thinking about this last night, now you're like our son!"

I went to the retreat with hopeful expectations, initially falling short. But glory to God who did more than I could have ever thought or asked for. My agenda was to make some friends. His agenda was to have me adopted into the family as a son. Before coming to UCSB, I prayed for one or two passionate, fiery Christian friends that I could do life with. Toward the end of my freshman year, I realized God answered that prayer. But He gave me more than one or two friends—He gave me a family.

THE HEART
OF A FATHER

SCOTT MARTINIS

When my parents started thinking about having children several years into their marriage, they began to research any potential complications or problems that could happen. Along the way, they discovered that a few rare and very debilitating genetic diseases ran in my mom's bloodline, and as a result, they risked having kids who would live their entire lives with a disability. However, those diseases can be detected in the child while still in the mother's womb, and if so, the parents can choose to abort the baby and save themselves a difficult life with a disabled child. In that time, my parents made an amazing choice. No matter what the test results showed, they would not abort their child. They decided then and there that they would unconditionally love their children no matter how hard or messy it would be.

One topic that receives a lot of attention in the church is submission to authority. One teacher I respect made a fascinating statement about submission: that submission to authority is about submitting to a father (or mother) figure who is completely committed to your well-being, not just obeying a person who is higher in church hierarchy than you are. To me, this is what fathering and mothering is about: spiritual and natural parents who decide they are willing to unselfishly suffer for the wellbeing of their children. To real fathers and mothers, their children's interests are more important than their own.

The most influential figures in my life have been men who have believed in me. When I was eight years old, my father took me to a conference on scientific reasons to believe in the existence of God. I was one of only a few children at the event, so most of the event was not geared toward my age group. My dad believed in me enough to bring me along with the expectation that I would understand enough to be impacted. That night at that conference I decided that God was real, and so I gave my life to Jesus.

In eighth grade I decided I wanted to become a Navy SEAL. I was at Barnes & Noble reading a book on Navy SEALs, and suddenly I decided that being a SEAL was what I wanted to do with my life. All that time reading Tom Clancy and other military books as a child helped me decide that I actually wanted to have a career in the military. So I went up to my dad and told him my decision.

Now, at that point, no one would have looked at me and said, "He is definitely going to become a Navy SEAL." I was chubby, not particularly athletic, and I had issues relating to people. However, my dad's first response to this statement was, "Well, you are smart, so if you want to become a SEAL, you should go to the Naval Academy." Fundamentally, my dad believed in me. He trusted that I could do what was necessary to actually achieve my dream. Currently, I am not a Navy SEAL, nor will I ever be. But the point is that my father, in spite of my physical and emotional stature, believed in the dreams I had.

I went to high school, began to run and get in shape, did well in school (due largely to the encouragement of my parents), and was eventually accepted to the Naval Academy. Many spiritual and natural parents were a part of this process; the more I look back on this time, the more I remember people who played a significant role. No one ever really makes it alone; the Holy Spirit always sends people to help and guide us into our dreams and destiny.

I went to the Naval Academy for two years, but I discovered a big disparity between how strong I thought I was and how strong I needed to be to become a Navy SEAL. During these years, I had a plethora of male authority figures modeling fathering in both good and bad ways. But eventually I found my way back to Santa Barbara and to ministry in Isla Vista, having learned so much in my journey with different mentors and father figures.

My life changed enormously through the love and belief my mentors had in me. After my freshman year, I considered leaving the Naval Academy for a while to do missionary work. These men taught me discernment and about following the will of God in a wise manner. I always struggled to fit in with groups, so another mentor helped me learn how to be a part of a community. He challenged my perceptions of who God is and what matters to Him, and simultaneously taught me about relationship with people while breaking the boxes I put God into. It was powerful to experience this man comfort me in my insecurity and still push me to go deeper in God.

However, despite all of these previous mentors, I still didn't understand covenant. I had not committed to serve any one of my spiritual father figures. At this point in my life, I was learning to hear God's voice and obey it on a moment-by-moment basis throughout my whole day. I spent most of my time hanging out with Him and practicing spiritual gifts. Though I grew in obedience, I lacked the knowledge and experience of covenantal relationship and submission among His believers.

Along the way, I started to spend more time with Jason. In the beginning of 2011, Jason and I met up for a class that the Isla Vista Church was hosting. The three-month class was "Prophecy, Healing, and Deliverance," which I happened to be doing a lot of at the time. Through these meetings I developed a relationship with Jason and began to trust him as a mentor and voice in my life. I thought about going to the Bethel School of Supernatural Ministry, but after multiple mentors suggested otherwise, I decided to stay in Santa Barbara.

As soon as I told Jason I wanted to stay in Santa Barbara, he offered me an internship at the Isla Vista Church. It was funny because he didn't view the internship as a functional thing; rather he viewed it more as spiritually adopting me. For most of my life, I felt disconnected from people, especially from groups, so Jason's offer to father me was quite amazing and something I'm still grasping. Jason didn't want another person to serve in the church, he simply wanted to love me and help me grow as a son.

Coming under Jason was a huge step for me because it meant commitment and covenant. If I didn't like what Jason said, or if I wanted to do something that he said no to, especially with regards to the church, I couldn't disobey. I had to submit, which was really good for me. However, Jason was very lenient with authority. He gave me freedom in ministry to be me and rarely told me what to do. There have been times of rebuke and confrontation, but Jason always acts with gentleness and kindness.

One fascinating thing about Jason's fathering is that he doesn't fix problems immediately. Primarily, he believes that Jesus "by one offering . . . perfected for all time those who are sanctified" (Hebrews 10:14

NASB). In others words, in Christ I am whole, perfect, and complete, so there is no longer anything fundamentally wrong with me.

One time I preached on the importance of not judging people, but in doing so I could tell my delivery was a bit harsh. I have a tendency to be hard on myself, and I could tell I made a mistake, so afterwards I asked Jason what I did wrong and what I could have done better. In retrospect, it was clear that I was a little too harsh, but I will never forget what he said in that moment, "You spoke from your heart, which was the important part." When I asked for specific correction, he refused to give it to me.

Part of fathering and mothering is knowing that children need time to grow. First and foremost, Jason believes in me. This is because he believes in Jesus and that Jesus is in me. When I make mistakes, Jason doesn't rush to fix me. He knows that God "predestined [me] to be conformed to the likeness of his Son" (Romans 8:29). Fundamentally, I am okay. True fathers trust their Father in Heaven to work things out. Jason doesn't have to fix everything he sees wrong immediately. He knows that as I walk with Jesus, God is maturing me as a son, and these issues often work themselves out over time.

Jason's faith in that has had enormous effects on the culture of the Isla Vista Church. He doesn't try to fix people, because he believes God has already given them a new nature. Ultimately, he trusts in God to work out all things as needed. As the people of our family experience Jason's faith in us, we are empowered to believe in others. It makes the family of God a restful thing because we no longer need to fix or change people; we are able to love and believe in people as they are. We don't have to worry about people or remind them of their shortcomings; because we love them, surface issues simply fade away.

I have a lot of dreams and goals I want to accomplish. Under Jason's leadership, if I wanted to create something but approach it without wisdom, he would say no to my plans while preserving my desires. Ultimately, he believes in me and wants to help me create with God, but part of his role is to help me remain on the path of wisdom. Sometimes I want to do things before I am ready or before others are ready, but Jason always speaks in a way that releases wisdom and safety, without attacking my heart or dreams.

One of the best and most enjoyable things we did together was create a discipleship program. Isla Vista Church had a traditional format for its School of Discipleship, and both of us felt God wanted something different for the next semester. Once we knew that was the case, we talked and brainstormed about how to change it. We decided to create a home group where people met up to read and discuss books together, with the goal of practically applying the books. It was awesome to create material for the home group because God gave us each three books that followed a logical progression and matched what we each felt God desired for our church body. Once the home group began, we realized that together we created something amazing.

One of the culminating points of the year was during a home group meeting as we went over *When Heaven Invades Earth* by Bill Johnson. Healing broke out, and several people in our church were healed. One girl had a partially deaf ear, and though we had prayed with her several times in the past, she finally began to experience healing in her ear that night. Nights like these didn't just randomly happen—God, Jason, and I created them together. Our partnership made it possible. Without the foundation of identity we laid at the home group months prior to this (coming from the books each of us separately received from God), people would have been unable to receive healing.

To me, Jason embodies what a father should be. A father should ultimately believe in his children and want them to grow into their dreams. A father should be able to give wisdom and rebuke gently, while not attacking his children or devaluing their hearts. Ultimately, a father's goal is to raise his children to be self-sufficient and able to govern their own lives. I love that Jason spiritually refuses to tie my shoes and forces me to go to God for myself. His favorite question is, "What is God saying to you?"

At the end of the day, of course, Jason is just following the example of my Father in Heaven, the Father of all. God always believes in me, He always has and He always will. It's astonishing, but God has nothing bad to say about me. By God's unchanging love and faithfulness, Jason has fathered me so that I can now father others.

CONCLUSION

JASON LOMELINO

I want to be frank to those reading this who currently are in the roles of spiritual fathers or mothers. The cry of the younger generation is to have older people in their lives. This generation is looking for those who have the desire to invest time, love, and energy into their lives. Don't be misled by the lack of church attendance, rebellious ways, or generational differences of tattoos, speech, or clothing that seem to suggest this younger generation has no need or want for you. God designed us for family and put in each of us an innate desire for older people to help us along and champion us in life.

Whenever I think about the needs of the church in America today, I can't think of a greater need than spiritual fathers and mothers. We need spiritual parents who are willing to discover that there is no greater joy than to see their children walk in the truth (3 John 1:4). The Old Testament ends with God making a promise to restore the hearts of the fathers to the children and the hearts of the children to the fathers (Malachi 4:6). The younger generation is fearful of authority and scared that anyone older than them will not value who they are or the dreams in their hearts. They are afraid that we will try to mold them into replicas of who we are and what we believe.

Instead, we need to be willing to spend time with them in order to genuinely understand their unique identity in Christ. Similar to parenting in the natural, there are basic guidelines for raising spiritual children. Anyone who has had more than one child knows that the wiring of the first child may be completely different than the second. But overall, the younger generation seeks to be understood, trusted, and believed in. Recently, I have been asked to sometimes include smiley-faces at the end of my text messages so some people can be assured of my tone when I write a message. This serves as a simple example of how authority can be scary in many ways, even when they know you are for them.

In Holly's chapter, she alluded to the sad fact that most people became wounded in their natural family. In their homes, they may have grown up with broken covenants, substance abuse, or parents with low emotional capacities to love or provide care. Circumstances such as these naturally lead to fear and lack of trust. Nevertheless, Jesus came to bring us back to our Father and to restore the word family for us. Because of this, I believe that the family of God is the remedy of heaven to heal the broken and to see health restored to this generation in Christ.

For far too long we have depended on sermons, Bible studies, and church programs to help fix problems that require far more than just knowledge. Undoubtedly, knowledge of God and His Word are vital for health, but this younger generation needs fathers and mothers who are willing to walk beside them with open hearts, not simply their knowledge. They need people that they feel safe with to talk about any area of their lives and be assured that their mess is not the end of the world. They always need to be reminded they are, in fact, going to be okay, are accepted, and that God has a plan for their life. They must be believed in and convinced that their best days await them. It is our role as fathers and mothers to impart faith, hope, and love into their life. We can no longer take them to church for a couple hours on Sunday, listen to another sermon and expect radical change; we must be involved and demonstrate to them a life lived with God.

People can sit for years in church racked with lies about themselves and God. All five of our spiritual children you just read about experienced this for themselves. They needed far more than a well-structured church full of good programs. They needed hands-on supportive parents in Christ who could help them see God in a clearer, more personal way and in turn understand their identity in Him. Both Brian and Scott's stories exemplify this, as each of them believed different lies about themselves that were holding them back from the fullness of their identity in Christ.

For Brian, he needed the breakthrough that took place at our church retreat to open up his heart to the Father more. He was in need of affection and the Father's embrace. Even since this retreat, Brian has walked up to me on multiple occasions and put his head on my chest. When I hug him, he just begins to cry, and I know the Father is bringing healing to his heart. It's amazing moments like these that have taught me a great deal about God as a caring, affectionate father. I had a good earthly father growing up, but the kind of affection I express toward Brian is something I had to learn and receive from relationship with Father God over years before I could give it to my natural and spiritual sons.

As for Scott, it has been a two-year journey of commitment to him that has allowed for my influence as a spiritual father to keep increasing in his life. His value for me gives me permission to speak truth into him and process the different seasons of life together that he experiences with God. Scott initially came to me hungry for fathering and mentoring. Similar to many, I doubt he knew what he really needed; he was just seeking more of God and saw something in me. However, God gave Scott what he wanted: covenant. A covenant is the only form of relationship that offers complete safety and security. When Scott understood that I was fully committed to him and that I was not going anywhere, he gained freedom. He became free to trust me more with his heart, life, and dreams, and gave me permission to speak into his choices and father him in various areas.

Spiritual parenting is comparable to driving a stick-shift car for the first time. You are nervous, have no clue what you are doing, and often find yourself driving in the wrong gear only to stall the car again and again. Holly and I have no desire to paint a glamorous picture of spiritual parenting. I can say with confidence that it isn't easy and we certainly don't have all the answers. We simply say yes to the children God sends us and then watch Him use this to further their journey while we receive the joy of seeing people walk in greater truth.

Living a life following Jesus makes you adequate for every opportunity that God places before you to love someone. I often remind the IV Church family that God is not looking for the gifted, just those who are willing to say yes to Him. When I first said yes to Jesus in 2001, I had no idea about the journey I was signing up for. I had no clue that when I gave my life to God, He would actually take it and form it into something that allowed others to grow from it one day. I assumed that I was becoming a better person who was experiencing a love that I never knew existed. But, thankfully, God had a bigger plan in mind that included other people I would invest my life in, and who would in turn invest their lives into others. Praise God that I said yes.

3

BOND THROUGH BATTLE

"FIGHT THE GOOD FIGHT OF FAITH; TAKE HOLD OF
THE ETERNAL LIFE TO WHICH YOU WERE CALLED."

—1 TIMOTHY 6:12 (NASB)

Bond Through Battle

Jason Lomelino

The reality of this world is that we are born into a war. It is an unseen war that has been taking place since the beginning of time. It is a war between good and evil, a war between the Kingdom of God and the kingdom of darkness. We have a real enemy and there are real casualties. In the heart of every believer is a desire to advance the Kingdom of God and to bring as many into it as possible, diminishing the domain of the devil and rescuing people from darkness. But it is not something we can do alone.

There is a bond that forms as we advance the Kingdom of God together. God doesn't send us alone into the battle of seeing a world come to know Him and be transformed into the image of His Son. The plans of God for His world, our cities, our churches, and our lives require more than our passive involvement. In John 17, Jesus prayed to the Father that we, His church, would be sent into the world just as His Father sent Him into the world. Living a life engaged in the battle is not something that only missionaries are called to do; it is something that every son and daughter is designed and destined to do. This will look different from one person to the next, though at the end of the day, it is our assignment from God to bring the culture of heaven to earth. Seeing the reign of God overcome the schemes and lies of the enemy is part of our inheritance as believers. While the war is real and there are genuine dangers and destruction, we are on the winning team and are assured of victory in Jesus. Prophesying of this, Isaiah the prophet said hundreds of years before the arrival of King Jesus, "Of the increase of his government and peace there shall be no end, upon the throne of David, and upon his kingdom, to order it, and to establish it with judgment and with justice from henceforth even for ever. The zeal of the LORD of hosts will perform this."

Over the years, I have discovered that some of the closest friendships are those that are formed while doing the work of the Kingdom together. My wife and I were first drawn to one another as friends because of our similar hearts for Isla Vista. We were both thankful to find someone else who wanted to labor together to see a city changed, and it didn't take long for us to become more closely bonded as we battled together for IV.

When we realize we have a common purpose and a common enemy, our unity becomes much stronger and more essential. In the early years of Isla Vista Church, many of us did not know each other very well. However, we had a desire to see the city of IV transformed for the glory of God. This common bond eventually became the basis for becoming family. Having something to fight for that was bigger than all of us rallied us to King Jesus and one another like nothing else could. Spending hours a week praying together, sharing the gospel, making Jesus Burgers, and loving a city knit our hearts to each other and kept Jesus the main thing. I have said often over the last decade that I could not be more thankful to live in a city that requires God to show up in such a real way, because if He didn't, nothing would change. This awareness of people needing to know Christ has caused people in the IV Church family, who would probably never associate with each other if they didn't know God, to actually live together and do life together, knowing their common bond was the exact same: Jesus and His Kingdom.

As in real life, going to battle is messy. Spiritual warfare is real, regardless if we acknowledge it or not. We must remember the battle is not always one you can readily see with the natural eyes. As the Apostle Paul said,

> For we are not fighting against flesh-and-blood enemies, but against evil rulers and authorities of the unseen world, against mighty powers in this dark world, and against evil spirits in the heavenly places (Ephesians 6:12 NLT).

The enemy hates those who are born in the image of God. His tactics always remain the same: divide and conquer; and his purposes are also always the same: steal, kill, and destroy. With that being said, we need to fight for one another. Death is almost certain for a soldier left alone on the battlefield, but a strong and united army is a powerful force to be reckoned with. We have to be willing to stand together and even be willing to lay down our lives for one another, just as Jesus did for us. The Apostle John could not have said it better in 1 John 3:16, "We know love by this, that He laid down His life for us; and we ought to lay down our lives for the brethren."

In the bond of family, we draw strength from one another to victoriously live in the battle at hand. We are feeding off of the life of God in each other. This bond of life is essential to our wellbeing and our victories in the Kingdom. God has not placed each of us in the world to be a one-man army; He has destined us to be a family of one man, Jesus. We need people around us who can give encouragement, impart strength, and spur us on toward lives of greater faith.

Family has taught me that I can no longer fight certain battles by myself; I need other people to fight with me. It is not healthy for me, nor is it as effective. For a long time in marriage, which carried into ministry, I thought if I just tried harder, read more, or prayed more, I could overcome my problems in life. It was not like those things were inherently wrong, as many of the things I did were good and aided my growth. However, what I have learned through trial and error is that what God desired to give me all along were others to strengthen my marriage, ministry, and life. God has designed the battle to need a bond to carry us onward to victory; it is all part of His master plan for holding us in relationship with Him and one another.

There is power in fighting together as a family. Jesus modeled the importance of gathering others to His side before going to battle against the enemy. Even though He defeated the enemy singlehandedly, He still refused to conquer the works of darkness by Himself. His mindset was to raise others up, to form a family that would fight together. He was the firstborn among many brethren, and as the firstborn, He demonstrated a new way of contending for the Kingdom of God. His role as the elder brother was to bring many sons and daughters to arms in the great battle of releasing His victory into the earth. The eternal purpose of God was to have a family, to bring the culture of heaven to earth, and for this invasion to be done as one united family full of faith in the impossible.

In my early years of reaching a city for His glory, it seemed like everyone was somewhat on his or her own team, trying to advance the Kingdom of God. It was apparent that if we walked in this independence and pride, we were not going to get much accomplished, and so we began working more as a single, unified team. But over the years, we have grown from a team mindset into a family. On a team, it is more about what you are trying to accomplish together rather than living in relationship with one another. That was very much how it was in the beginning. God brought a small band of us together with a heart for Isla Vista, and our bond centered on seeing people in the city come to know Him. It didn't take long to begin experiencing how much the enemy did not like this plan. And so we found ourselves in a battle. The warfare was real and often constant. But it was through this raging battle that God in His infinite wisdom began to bind us in a much deeper way. It required both a deeper experience of the goodness and love of God as well as a more real and powerful love for one another. And with each battle fought and victory won, we came out that much closer and bonded on the other side. We began to experience what it was to be a family, to fight for one another no matter what and to love regardless. Now as a family, it is more about the unconditional love of the Father emanating through us to one another, and a desire to see that same love conquering the fear and darkness on the earth.

FREELY
YOU HAVE
RECEIVED,
FREELY GIVE

TARRA RARICK

I spent a lot of time with my family as a little girl. Whenever it was just my dad and I, he would teach me about history, the stock market, and Jesus. Not surprisingly, my earliest encounter with God happened on one of those nights hanging out while he explained the moment that the Father turned his face away from Jesus on the cross. I could see the deep joy and thankfulness in my dad's heart through the tears that began to stream down his face. So in love with this God I hardly knew, I wept into my pillow. My mom walked in wondering what in the world was happening, and I quickly wiped away my tears, not sure what to think myself. All I knew was this Jesus man was my friend who died because He really loved me. I was just a little nine-year-old girl experiencing God's presence for the first time, and it laid the foundations of my faith for the rest of my life.

My relationship with God never ended, but it never really grew either. My parents did a remarkable job of loving me and raising me to stand on my own feet, but in order to grow spiritually I needed to be surrounded by people who would constantly push me toward the fullness of Jesus. I couldn't imagine what such an extraordinary community like that would look like, and it wasn't until my first year of college at UC Santa Barbara that God spoke to my heart and called me to stop running for the world and start running after him. The funny thing is, after surrendering all of my ambitions, He gave me more joy and purpose than I could have imagined, and it came in the form of a radical Spirit-filled family: Isla Vista Church.

On one of my first visits to Isla Vista Church (IVC) there was dinner afterward at Pastor Jason's house just down the street. Claire, my bible study leader at the time, had asked if Jason and three other girls could pray and prophesy over me, and I gladly received their offer. Despite not knowing me too well, they responded in selfless love by praying for me, and because they were so sincere and gentle I easily trusted them to take on my burdens. I felt valued and cared for just knowing that each of them stopped the conversations they were having outside to come into the house and give me their undivided attention.

After a couple minutes of praying, Cassie asked me if I had a younger sister to which I responded yes. Having no previous knowledge of my life (I just met her that night), she confidently told me that my sister looked up to me more than I knew. I immediately burst into tears, and all the guilt I secretly felt in my relationship with my sister melted into hope. Then another girl said she had a vision of me running freely through a meadow, a vision that helped confirm decisions she didn't even know I was trying to make. The accuracy of these words made me trust in this family even more, and I left that little living room knowing something new: God likes to speak to us, and He will use family to do it.

Before that weekend, I was already attending another local church, and I went to IVC only if I finished my homework. But after experiencing the closeness of the smaller family atmosphere in Jason's home, I had a feeling this community was more than a weekly event to simply attend. After a service one Sunday at IVC, I rushed over to Mac, the worship pastor, and asked him to pray for me to know God better. With a cheerful smile on his face he prayed, and then he had me sit down, open my hands, and simply repeat, "I receive."

When I went up for this prayer, I was desperate for intimacy with God, and I put myself in a vulnerable position by asking for help to get it. Despite how little I knew about the Bible and how immature my request could have sounded, Mac did not judge me, but loved me, looked at me through the Father's eyes, listened to the Father's voice, and helped me to receive all that God had for me.

In retrospect I think that Mac prophetically symbolized Isla Vista Church in my life. I saw that Mac understood God's heart and experienced an intimate friendship with Him that I wanted for myself, so I came to him in the same way I eventually came to IVC and felt fully accepted and free to be where I was. Through this small but meaningful interaction with the family, I realized two foundational concepts that further pushed me toward community: we must be willing to wait on God, and we cannot give love until we first receive His love. As I spent more time at IVC, I began receiving great revelation and close relationship and soon chose it to be my permanent church. That summer I knew this was my home. Instead of offering weekly accountability partners, this family commits to being brothers and sisters as God's beloved children seeking His kingdom and glory in this city.

Soon I was at the Jesus Burgers ministry every

Friday night, eager to be out on the street with the family and our favorite party people. One of the most incredible nights I've ever had out there showed me the importance of selflessly devoting your time, energy, and love to others just like the IVC family did for me. It began around midnight with a guy named Dave, whom I met at the fire pit. He was high on cocaine, and I listened closely as he struggled to tell me about the good times and hardships of his life before he left to see his friends.

Around two o'clock a.m., the burger grill was already shut down, and I was ready to walk home when another one of my friends, Luis, called me and wanted to talk in front of the Jesus Burger house. He began to tell me about some demonic oppression he had been experiencing, when IVC family members Scott, Israel, and Kristin stopped to say goodnight to us before we headed home. They decided to stay with us, and we all ended up talking and praying for over an hour, delivering Luis from several unclean spirits and encouraging him with loving words.

Somewhere in that time frame a random guy running down the street came up to us and asked if we had any marijuana. Scott excitedly offered him the Holy Spirit instead, and his only response was, "Well, I'm drunk. Might as well!" Our new friend, Devon, sat with us and within ten minutes was sober, got his shoulder healed, received specific words of knowledge, and wanted nothing to do with the weed he first approached us for. Meanwhile, Luis watched in awe as this guy got transformed before his very eyes.

Luis had to go home, so we continued talking to Devon when all of a sudden, at about four o'clock a.m., Dave returned to the fire pit again and said, "I felt like I should come back here." Kristin, Israel, and I simply listened to him talk and speak love and freedom from addiction over his life while Scott led Devon through some inner healing, let him confess his sins, and left him to talk to God on his own for a while. After about ten minutes of personal prayer, Devon sat up and told Scott he wanted Jesus in his heart. Scott, in a state of ecstatic bliss, explained baptism to him, and Devon agreed to get dunked in the ocean across the street at five o'clock a.m.! Dave left to go home soon after that, so we ran to the beach and found them just getting out of the water, shouting in celebration of new life. I asked Devon how he felt, and he said with a look of awe on his face, "I feel like I can love again."

Love definitely won that battle. In the midst of all that happened, there was a moment when I realized that the four of us would have done literally anything for these young men. Fighting for God's Kingdom simply meant listening to them, praying for them, and sacrificing some sleep, a small price to pay to show them God unconditionally loves them.

I am so thankful that Scott, Israel, and Kristin were willing to lay down their lives that night because it confirmed in my heart that this family is fully committed to serving and loving *all* of God's people *all* of the time. Together we accomplish things that I could never do alone. Isla Vista Church fought for me and took me in as family. Because of that, my heart's desire is to demonstrate that same love to everyone in this city.

AN ARMY FOR ONE MAN

CONNOR MULLEN

Growing up, I could say that I was raised in a typical Christian family. I went to church every Sunday, had parents that loved each other and God, and asked for forgiveness for my sins before bed each night. More routine than anything, I went through the motions week in and week out all throughout my upbringing. I never developed a relationship with God, as I found Christianity to be fake and boring. It wasn't until the summer of my junior year of college that I encountered the power of God on a mission trip to Brazil. I was praying for a blind woman during one of the evening services, and she was healed on the spot. It blew me away and changed everything, or so I thought. However, throughout college I never had fruitful community, which would have helped foster and blossom this experience. Instead, I had quite the opposite and tried to go at it alone, with dismal results.

Entering my senior year of college, I lived with the same roommates I had for the past year and a half, four non-Christian guys. The only thing we did on Sunday was recover from the previous night's party. We never interacted on any meaningful level; we all just lived from one thrill to another. God was the furthest thing from my mind, and it wasn't until I had a crazy encounter with Him my second semester that He started to come into the picture again. His timing was perfect. If that encounter did not happen, I probably would not have come back to a relationship with God.

I have been an introvert for as long as I can remember. While some people get their energy from being in groups, I am the opposite. It's more the one-on-one interactions that bring me to life. Over the years, God has brought me into battling for the Kingdom with others instead of being a one-man army. He is growing my heart to join with others to contend for cities as well as growing my patience to bring back stray sheep to the flock, while empowering them in the process.

When I returned from Brazil, after seeing incredible healings, I got plugged into IV Church, where along with meeting many people, I also met Carsten, Scott, and Kyle. Together, we went out on the streets of downtown Santa Barbara to demonstrate the love of God and pray for the sick. At that point in time, I was the only one in the group who had seen miracles and not just heard about them. Leading a group like this was not in my nature. It felt awkward at first, having day after day go by without seeing any breakthrough in miracles. Were they questioning what I actually saw in Brazil? I even started to question what I saw, asking God why we saw no breakthrough in the streets. The response I got was, "wait." So I chose to trust God even though I felt uncomfortable and questioned His nature. Throughout our contending for breakthrough in the streets, our relationships grew as we spent more time together. We would soak in God's presence and pray for Him to open doors.

We spent roughly a month going out on the streets, and over the entire course of that time we did not see a single miracle. It actually wasn't until I went back to school that the three guys saw breakthrough. Looking back, God was growing our relationships first and knew that if we saw miracles right away, we might take them for granted after a while. I know now that it was God's plan for me to bond with these guys through contending for the city. As I grew in intentionality with these guys, God stirred my heart not only to contend for the city, but for each other as well. Recently, He used the battle over the spirit of isolation in a brother to bring him from a wandering sheep to a member of the family.

In any church, there are always people on the outskirts who don't quite feel like they fit in. For whatever reason, the pieces don't line up. God has put it on my heart to go after these people. I can relate because I used to be in their shoes. Within the past year, God has brought one person in particular to me, Chris. The timing of having him enter my life was impeccable, almost textbook. It occurred halfway through a year of living in an environment of strong brotherly community, and marked a shift in the dynamic of the house. God had prepared me for this transition during the first part of the year. It was as if I had gone through a boot camp of sorts, and without knowing, I was suddenly thrown into the battlefield. Slightly confused at first, God's purpose for this change started to become very clear through prayer.

He wanted me to fight with Chris to free him from the spirit of isolation. Initially, I thought "no way, God." So many others had tried, and I thought, "What do I have to offer that they don't?" At first, our interactions didn't yield much fruit, as I wasn't being fully intentional in spending time with Chris. It felt very taxing as I didn't feel like hanging out sometimes, but I noticed that in any given situation when I felt like leaving, if I would press in further, God would give me more patience and a greater capacity to love. It almost feels opposite of what you would expect to happen, but we serve a God who equips us to battle any situation that we are presented with. I set out to be intentional in my relationship with this brother, and set aside time during each week to hang out and spend quality time with him.

With each passing time we spent, I was able to hear his heart more as well as share mine, and come alongside him in his battle over isolation. Victories were had as well as some defeats, but in the end, the smallest of victories are worth any number of defeats. As life threw curveballs at both of us, we bonded over talking and coming alongside each other battle after battle. Chris became more empowered as a child of God in his own identity, and I got to see him grow with each passing day. I could have spent my time pursuing a plethora of other things, but I know God set up the living situation to have me shepherd a part of the flock that, well, didn't feel a part of the flock any longer.

My time with the IVC family has shown me that battling for the Kingdom with others bears more fruit than doing it alone. Whether it is battling for a city with fellow brothers, or intentional one-on-one relationships to bring MIA brothers back into the family, there is power in the bond. We share our burdens and our victories, as there is strength in numbers. In the midst of battle, our bonds empower us to never give up, never surrender.

CONTENDING
FOR FAMILY

ANDY DO

Ever since I was little, God placed in my heart this deep longing for "the perfect family." I have always had a strange fascination with the idea of family. I would watch movies like *Home Alone*, where I would see families gather by the fireside. There was an unspoken understanding of true family. I would observe the closeness of my friends' families. They had a love for each other that was so real. Growing up, my family at home was completely the opposite. As long as I can remember, my parents have always fought back and forth, constantly yelling at each other in the house. Unfaithfulness, lack of trust, and constant miscommunication had left a complete sense of brokenness in my family life. Not only that, I cussed at my parents, told them I hated them, and was constantly disrespectful and condescending toward them; there was a clear lack of affection and love toward one another. I had so much regret in my heart. I wanted to tell them that I loved them, but this barrier of awkwardness always prevented me from stepping over the line and saying it. Every night when I prayed to God, I would say, "If mom or dad died tomorrow in a car accident or some other way, I will have regret for the rest of my life because I never told them or showed them that I love them."

The summer before my freshman year of college I had a powerful supernatural encounter with God at a Charismatic Catholic Healing Mass, and it catalyzed my hunger for more of God. But it was later in the year at UCSB that I actually met Jesus. As I came to know the Lord during those early years of college, God began to reconcile relationships in my family. My relationship with my parents began to flourish and grow stronger, as I consistently prayed for God's healing to restore our broken family. I could see God starting to move in my relationship with my parents, but my family as a whole was still shattered and disconnected. I realized that without the love of Jesus, it would be impossible for our family to be whole again. I was still searching, still desiring in my heart for God to give me that "perfect family."

While attending UCSB, God provided me with two amazing Christ-centered communities, Campus Crusade for Christ and Isla Vista Church. Going to UCSB and living in Isla Vista for the past five years has spoiled me socially. There are always friends and church family that I can fall back on and always something to do or someone's house to visit. In each of these years, including now, I have lived in community houses/dorms and been surrounded by Christians who love Jesus. My favorite year of living in community was by far living at the Del Playa House last year (2011–2012). There was so much laughter in the house and everyone got along without drama. All of us were good friends, and we loved hanging around one another. Whenever describing my living situation to other people, I like to say, "I feel like I'm living in heaven on earth." Because I had so much fun living there, I wouldn't describe being on the front line on DP a "battlefield." Usually people living in Christian community say, "Man, it was SO, SO, SO hard to live there, but we grew so much." But I literally felt like I was in a Jesus resort on a year long vacation. I am so blessed that the Lord allowed us to experience such amazing fellowship together and have supernatural social connections.

However, though our home was socially amazing, I felt like we could have definitely fellowshipped in the Spirit with one another more. We had a lot of fun together and shared many laughs, but in my heart there was something missing, and I still wondered what that "true family" really looked like.

Jesus said, "If two of you on earth agree about anything you ask for, it will be done for you by my Father in Heaven" (Matthew 18:19). Said another way, if two or more harmonize in the Spirit on anything, it will be done for them. My roommate, Justin, and I are such completely different people. If it weren't for Jesus, we probably would not be hanging out with each other. As far as hobbies and interests go, we are almost perfect opposites. But in the things of the Spirit, we are able to connect on a level that is rare for most people.

Isaiah Saldivar spoke at the Upper Room one Friday night, and the power of God flowed in the meeting in such a powerful way. Instead of staying for Jesus Burgers, Justin and I drove down to Orange County to visit our families. During the drive, we literally had two and a half hours of straight intercession. I don't know how to describe it, but it was like the anointing of the Holy Spirit leaked out onto us. The two hours felt like fifteen minutes, and we could have kept going for the rest of the night.

Even though we don't have a lot of other things in common, we bonded that night in such a deep and powerful way through prayer. The harmony in the

Spirit was powerful and tangible. We knew nations were being changed and shifted through our prayers that night, and God felt so real and near. We didn't do anything special that night, nor did we pray any differently than at any other prayer meetings. There was simply a supernatural grace and anointing that came over us for intercession; it was nothing we earned. I would choose to have one night of that kind of bonding over one million nights of fun board games and movies. Bonding over games, movies, sports, and other hobbies is great, but experiencing the closeness of brotherhood through prayer is incredibly special and way beyond anything else I have ever encountered.

Intercession is just one example of how I was able to get a glimpse of the true, intimate family that I've wanted my whole life. There have been other random times in my walk with God when I've felt that same intimate unity from bonding in prayer. Bonding came mostly through interceding for redemption for our natural families, for salvation in Isla Vista and the nations. We would pray from a place of pure brokenness and compassion because of seeing the pain, loss, and suffering in our own families and the people in the streets of Isla Vista.

I have regularly interceded for my family, for IV, and for this nation throughout my walk as a believer. Even so, I am still in the process of seeing the results of what I am contending for. My family is far from completely being restored, and IV still has yet to see massive revival sweep the city. But I am only twenty-three, and I have been praying for only a handful of years. Men and women of faith have contended their whole lives, risking everything to see the Word of the Lord fulfilled. They have sacrificed their whole lives for fruit that they wouldn't get to see in their lifetime. Even Abraham didn't get to see the fulfillment of God's promise to him that his descendants will be as numerous as the stars in the sky (Genesis 26:4).

I wait with my brothers and sisters to see the fulfillment of our prayers and His promises. In the bonds that have been formed through intimate moments with God and one another in prayer, I have seen a glimpse of the authenticity of true family.

I have not seen the complete fulfillment of many of the things I have prayed for, but I know that God has heard every single one of those prayers. I believe that He will completely restore and save my natural family, and that He will bring many people of IV into the family of God. In my journey of discovering the true meaning of family, I am so blessed to know the bond that comes through praying with my brothers and sisters in Christ. God has called His family to pray, and I am privileged to answer His call with this family.

HE'S
WORTH IT

KRISTIN STRITZEL

I grew up in a traditionally Catholic family, believing in God and doing religious works simply to earn His love and get into Heaven. I was never aware that Jesus actually wanted to have a relationship with me. I had many false idols including school, body image, and partying. I was living to impress others.

Once I came to college, I gave in to the temptations of the world and partying became one of my main activities as I conformed to a life of excessive drinking and trying to impress others. I am not going to act like it wasn't fun, because I did enjoy it most of the time. During my freshman year of college I did well in school and went to Catholic Mass every Sunday. I thought my church fix justified the partying I did on the weekends. However, God as a Friend and Father was never part of my life. As school became more demanding during my sophomore year, my partying began to spiral out of control.

Drinking and cavorting became the norm for me, and my body image worsened because of it. I was never satisfied with my body; I let my weight determine my happiness. I always felt the need to skip a meal before drinking or not eat at all that day. I would weigh myself every day, and that number would determine what I would eat for the day. It was a sick obsession. The only calories I enjoyed consuming were from alcohol. Partying was the way I could bond with my roommates and feel the affirmation I craved.

I remember many of my housemates coming home with stories of what they did with other guys from the night before. Sex and hooking up seemed like a rewarding and prideful experience for them, and I wanted that. I felt the need to feel experienced and hook up with guys because I had never had a boyfriend. This led me to believe that I was not good or pretty enough for others. My nights usually consisted of drinking so much that I would black out and maybe kiss a guy, wake up limping with bruises on myself, or find out I had vomited and did not remember it. I took pride in my drinking and thought the things that happened to me were hilarious. Floatopia, a spring festival and another excuse to party in IV, was when my drinking took a turn for the worse. That was the day I lost my virginity.

I remember leaving the room after, in recognition of my black out, and feeling embarrassed, ashamed, and worthless. Why had this felt so rewarding for others but not for me? Why did I not feel accomplished? In shock, I did not want to tell anyone what had just happened. I sat on the curb feeling lonelier then ever. Even with the circumstances alcohol put me in, I still continued to find my worth in it.

After some time, I began to realize that there was no meaning to my life, and I finally noticed the emptiness I felt. Living in a house of ten girls where we all lived to party had only encouraged me to keep up with all of my embarrassing stories. It wasn't until Halloween weekend after partying my junior year of college that I truly encountered the love of God and decided to live for something greater than myself.

I was first introduced to IVC through my former housemate, Heather. As soon as I entered the church, the pastor, Jason, came up to me and introduced himself. I felt so loved and important just because the pastor made a point to know me. At the end of church, everyone began praying and prophesying over one another, and the words that Jason spoke over me truly hit my heart. I couldn't believe how well God knew and loved me. That day, I instantly fell in love and knew that IVC was going to be my home church. It amazes me how IVC is based on family and doing life with each other. As soon as I became part of the family, I was hungry for more of God and desired to bless people and become more and more intimate with God.

For the first six months of my walk with God, I still lived in the house with twelve other girls, most of whom I used to party with. My home was a spiritual battleground, and it was extremely difficult. There were many nights I could not sleep because of people hooking up in my room, yelling and screaming, or the music blasting into the early hours of the morning. I experienced demonic oppression in my dreams, and I would often have to sleep with my twin sister, who also lived in Isla Vista. I had to keep reminding myself that I used to party, too, and that my housemates were not hurting me on purpose. It was hard for me to love them when I was going through all of this spiritual warfare.

Living in that house stunted the growth of my relationship with God and becoming more aware of His voice, giving me great frustration. I felt the only way to grow with God was to avoid the house by leaving every weekend while they would party.

As a Christian, knowing that we can hear the Father is one of the most powerful truths, and that is why our confidence in hearing Him gets attacked so frequently. Heather has been amazing and encouraging in this area of my walk with God. Learning to have confidence in hearing the Shepherd's voice has sustained me in times when I felt attacked and alone without community while living in that house. Whenever I felt unworthy or like I couldn't hear God, she would read me scriptures that stated otherwise, and we would prophesy over each other. I did not have to pretend like I was fine around Heather or the IVC family, because it was a place to be completely honest and vulnerable.

I realized that in times of trial you really need family. Whenever times would be shaky with the roommates, I would turn to my IVC family or go to Jason's house and ask for prayer. It is such a blessing to have a pastor who cares enough to be involved in every family member's life. Though I had little support from my roommates, I knew I had a family who loved me and would care for me. Because of the encouragement I received from the IVC family, I was able to grow in my walk with God. Before long, I was committed to ministry at the spiritual encounter sign on Friday nights during Jesus Burgers.

One night at the spiritual encounter sign, Scott asked me to pray for a boy's leg to grow out. I prayed, and his leg grew out and his spine straightened! The guy even tested out his spine by lying down. Before this night, I believed in miracles and prophecy, but for some reason I never believed that Jesus could work through me to make those miracles happen. Soon after this, Jessica, Israel, Bridget, and I decided to commit to the sign and help Scott demonstrate God's Kingdom on Del Playa. There were times when

I felt unequipped to pray for healing or give a word of knowledge to someone, but it was so incredibly encouraging to have four people by my side to push me to step out in faith. Other times, there would be so many people coming up to the sign that it was necessary to have a person nearby to pray or prophesy with. No matter what the situation was, I had to rely fully on Jesus to provide, and of course He always did.

Crazy things happened at the sign. Billy was healed of arthritis in his hands. Naran's back was partially healed, and he was super encouraged to start going back to church. Sydney was healed of scoliosis. Sarah had a bump on her back, and it shrunk. Kenny got healed of a headache and sinus pain. David's knee and shoulder pain supernaturally vanished. Caleb got healed of sinus problems in his broken nose. Meredith had a bone protruding out of her foot, and Jesus healed her. One boy named Devon was visiting from Los Angeles and got physically healed, heard the gospel, received accurate prophetic words, gave his life to Jesus, and got baptized in the ocean all in one night. These testimonies are just a taste of what Jesus does on Friday nights at Jesus Burgers.

Committing to the sign not only blesses people on DP but also equips each of us at the sign to be bold and trust God even more. Battling for the city at the spiritual encounter sign has taught me to trust in my family and turn to them when I need encouragement. As they surrounded me with support, I kept fighting for God's Kingdom. Because they saw me how God sees me, I was able to accept for myself that I am made in God's perfect image, and I was then able to see my housemates in that same light. By the end of the year, I was spending more time with them and actually wanted to come home for parties on the weekends.

I eventually learned how to bring Jesus to the house and love my roommates as Jesus does. The same love I gave to God's children on DP was brought into my home. I prayed for healing and gave prophetic words to some of my housemates. There are no limits to God. Because He lives inside of us, anything can happen anytime, anywhere. Though my relationships with my roommates are not the same as they once were, I know that living for Jesus is worth it all. Now, I have the amazing privilege and joy of loving and treating my former housemates, family, and friends the way God does, as royalty!

There is nothing like having a family to turn to whenever I feel down or incapable. Because of the IVC family and my commitment to the sign, I am equipped to fight for God's Kingdom and experience intimacy with the Father.

I owe it all to Scott, the leader of this spiritual encounter sign ministry, as well as Heather, who had faith in me and encouraged me to do what I was made for: to love people. Now, I have no doubts about who I am and what I am capable of doing through Jesus inside of me.

CONCLUSION

LUCAS BELL

The battle is not to be fought alone. The bond of family strengthens us to fight the good fight. God is not seeking to train soldiers to take orders; rather He wants a family of bonded warriors who are well equipped for battle. In the safety of bonded relationships, individuals craft their instruments of war. For many, this means stepping into their identity as a champion of God and stepping out in faith. We continually find ourselves in the midst of a raging battle for the hearts of mankind. This is not a battle that we can easily walk away from without dismissing Jesus' great commission to make disciples of all nations. Jesus said we would accomplish this, and He gave us each other to do it with. The family of God is His royal army, commissioned to destroy the works of the devil. The New Testament is filled with encouragement toward the saints as they fight the good fight and engage in the warfare at hand. God uses family to create a safe community where we can actively advance His Kingdom together.

God is creating a family of believers that knows the power of Christ's finished work, the victory of the cross. He is gathering together a unified community whose purpose is to release the victory of Jesus into any and every circumstance. Every member of the family is designed and destined to engage in the battle at some level. Furthermore, we are promised to celebrate in Christ's glorious victory. With each battle we are presented with the opportunity to experience His victory. He places us in family in hopes that this reality will be ingrained into our daily lifestyle, calling us to celebrate the victory of His Son as our own.

Spiritual family is designed to draw strength from one another. We serve as a hub for the life of God to flow to and from. Our spirits must have this life if we are going to be victorious in the battles we are called to face. We draw strength from one another as we do life together. This strength will permeate into the battles that He calls us to fight, equipping us as sons and daughters of the King.

Every battle needs a bond, but not every bond needs a battle. God, in His infinite wisdom, designed battles in hopes of bonds being formed. God always wants us to fight from the fullness of His love, which we can experience in family. Family teaches us to receive God's love, contend for each other, and manifest His worth. Fathers, mothers, brothers, and sisters all bond together, as they believe in the impossible and see heaven come forth.

Family taught Tarra the necessity of being friends with God and receiving His love. She craved intimacy with God, and through her brothers and sisters, she understood that it was possible to experience God's love for herself. Soon, she was empowered to minister to other people from a place of overflowing love. She learned to receive God's love before she gave it away. In relationship, she found her bond with God and became a powerful minister of the Gospel. Her life is now filled with testimonies of advancing God's Kingdom. Family fought for her, and now she fights for others to know the life changing power of the love of God. As we advance the Kingdom, God will strategically place individuals in our lives that He is calling us to bond with. These bonds are gifts of God that will do more for His Kingdom than we could ever do alone.

Connor experienced the closeness of companionship on the front lines. He set out to demonstrate God's love and power, yet he ended up discovering the importance of having relationships first. Through fighting for a city, he discovered the need to contend for each other. He transitioned from a one-man army to an army for one man—Jesus. Connor's heart for breakthrough continues to fuel his love for both cities and individuals. As we advance the Kingdom of God, we will face battles that need our bond in Jesus. Family presents us with a community of like-minded people that often shares similar passions and desires for the Kingdom. From this place, we have the opportunity to become more than soldiers. As family, we become an army of God.

Although we may not come from the ideal family, God knows the desires of our hearts. He sees our longings to live with an intentional community. In this community, we can develop our hunger to see the world changed for the glory of God. As we do life together, we must place a high value on the power of prayer. Andy experienced the joy of living in authentic Christian community, but he also saw the need for prayer. For him, the battle began and ended in prayer. Through prayer, he bonded with other brothers, as their hearts shared a common cry. God fulfilled Andy's longing for family through the bond of intercession. Prayer is a language that enables the family to speak to God and to one another. It is a safe place for people to connect and contend. From the strength of their connection, they draw life to contend for the deeper things of God. In the presence of family, God manifests himself. The family must only ask God and agree together for heaven to come to earth.

God also uses family to give us the affirmation we often crave, to tangibly bond us to His love. Formerly, Kristin sought for the world to meet her needs, but then she encountered the love of God and was brought into family. She quickly discovered that He is worth her entire life. Her bond with fellow brothers and sisters ultimately taught her how to be in a relationship with God. In this safe place, she learned to hear God's voice, to be honest and vulnerable before others, and to minister the Gospel through the power of Christ. Her bond in family empowered her to fight for the Kingdom of God, teaching her faith, hope, and love. She now believes in the power of Christ within her. She has committed herself to others for the common purpose of advancing the Kingdom, and now she sees powerful miracles on a regular basis. God knows that we need to be bonded in family in order to enter the good fight of faith. Together, we discover the worth that He has given us in His Son, which empowers us to reveal and foster that in others.

Bonds are formed, strengthened, and tested in the midst of battle. Our union with Christ gives us an eternal bond that no battle can stand against. Our individual bonds with Christ will form into an anchor of love as we advance the Kingdom together. God's heartbeat is union. From the bond of His Trinity, He sent Christ to defeat sin and death. Now the power of the resurrected Christ rests in the bond of family. His love has bonded us to our Father and to each other, equipping and propelling us into the battle. The bond of family, "endures everything without weakening; its hopes are fadeless under all circumstances" (1 Corinthians 13:7).

4

FOSTERING CHAMPIONS

"BUT ENCOURAGE ONE ANOTHER DAY AFTER DAY, AS
LONG AS IT IS STILL CALLED 'TODAY,' SO THAT NONE OF
YOU WILL BE HARDENED BY THE DECEITFULNESS OF SIN."

—*HEBREWS 3:13 (NASB)*

FOSTERING CHAMPIONS

JASON LOMELINO

The family of God is designed to raise champions that not only advance the Kingdom of God here and now but also reign in the life to come. A champion, by definition, is a warrior, a fighter. The Bible declares in Jeremiah 20:11 that God is like a dread champion, "But the LORD is with me like a dread champion; therefore, my persecutors will stumble and not prevail." Jesus is the Champion of champions, King of kings, and Lord of lords. He made us to reign in the earth and in the age to come. In many ways, we are training for reigning in this life, learning how to walk as a champion of the ultimate Champion. God intended His family to be a safe place for sons and daughters to be empowered as champions as they grow into their God-given destiny.

Fostering a culture of champions begins with establishing identity and security in the heart of each person within the family of God. In my own life, I have seen firsthand that without understanding who I am in Christ, I am a sitting duck for the enemy, completely vulnerable to the lies he wants to sow into my heart. In order to create a culture of fostering champions, we must view people the way God views them. Like Jeremiah the prophet, we must be able to extract the precious from the worthless in the lives of those around us (Jeremiah 15:19). It doesn't take a supernatural gifting to see and speak of the junk in each other's lives; however, it does take eyes of faith, hope, and love to see the champion that someone is becoming. In over a decade of pastoring and watching a family form, I can honestly say that partnering with God in speaking out people's potential rather than shortcomings has had one of the greatest impacts in securing them in Christ.

Like Gideon, David, Peter, and so many others throughout Scripture, God spoke to who they really were in His sight; He did not address who they were not. Champions are not born; they are made. They are made by God and fostered by the family. Everyone needs to be championed by those around them. This may mean helping someone realize that they are worthy of God's love or reassuring them that they can do what God has placed before them. Either way, we need to be encouraged by those around us. Literally, we must be given courage to face the giants in our lives and courage to go after the desires in our hearts.

For most, that giant is fear: fear of the unknown, fear of not being able to do something, or fear of what others may think. To diminish fear and release faith, we must be believed in and empowered by family. We must be convinced that we are not alone. Just as Jesus believed in Peter to walk on water, we need to know that we were born to get out of the boat and take a risk at the impossible. We must be spoken into with words of life and given opportunities to look fear in the face and choose to move forward.

Providing an atmosphere of safety and empowerment has been an unarticulated goal of mine over the years. I never sought out to do this, yet by beholding Jesus and discovering the safety of the Father and the power of the Spirit, this kind of environment emerged. This environment has helped secure people, while simultaneously releasing them to obtain their heart's greatest desires.

In order to lead a church and foster leaders, I have adopted a core value that everyone is amazing, yet accountable to one another. Not accountable in the traditional Christian accountability, which for the most part says, "I am watching you, so don't do that." The kind of accountability I am referring to in fostering champions says, "What is in your heart to do, and how can I get behind you to do that?" Like David, it was in his heart to build a temple for God, a dwelling place or resting place for the presence. We, as the church, need a new kind of accountability where people become accountable to the abilities that God has given them. For some, it is addressing issues in their lives that are hindering the purposes of heaven from coming forth; for others, it is giving them a grid for faith and patience to see the promises emerge in their lives; and often for others, it is being a stable rock in their lives that genuinely and sincerely believes in who they are in God. Leadership holds people accountable to the destiny and desires of God.

I have learned over the years that the goal of good leadership is not to get others to serve our vision; it is to discover the vision in those whom we are leading and release them to fulfill the desires that God has put in their hearts. Champions emerge as we give them opportunities to step into the potential that God has given them. We are providing wind for their sails to begin or to continue the voyage that God has them on. We are creating pioneers and forerunners instead of servants or good employees.

We have a gathering called the Upper Room on Friday nights before Jesus Burgers. Over the last five years, I have found key leaders I believed God was calling to steward this time. The structure has changed each year due to the various individuals God has called to lead this gathering. As Lead Pastor of the church, I could have easily told whoever was leading the Upper Room what we were going to do and how it should look. Because of my role, this would have worked. However, God never asked me to be the type of church CEO that determines what is going to happen and what is not. Instead, He asked me to be a father who is called to release sons and daughters to do what is in their heart for their King.

In the context of family, a CEO kind of structure gives the emerging leader no opportunities to release what God has put in their heart. They are given a mold to lead from rather than freedom to follow the Spirit. This mold may or may not draw out the potential that God has deposited in them. Most often though, following such rigid guidelines for leadership kills the life of God, as does following the letter of the law without the Spirit. When growing leaders are given an environment of empowerment, freedom, and accountability, there is opportunity for growth, fulfillment, and life. This life then morphs naturally into the God-ordained church structure, instead of a manufactured one. Like pre-packaged processed food, this manufactured structure may be easier and less messy, but at the end of the day, it lacks the nutrients of homegrown, organic food from your own garden.

Life produces church structure; structure does not produce life. Creating champions means appointing leaders and giving them opportunities to lead. Over the years, people outside of our church family have asked me countless times, "What is your vision?" It always makes me chuckle inside, as I know they want a long explanation of my mission and goals. For me, it is not so much a matter of executing *my* vision as it is partnering with those God has brought me into relationship with. From the life of our relationships we create a structure, which both stewards His heart for the city and empowers each other to fulfill the visions that God has placed in us. Like relationships, visions work in favor of each other.

I strongly believe, as the Word affirms, that the Holy Spirit places people in the family of God according to His pleasure. As leaders and overseers, it is our privilege to give away the ministry to others because we believe that God puts individuals in our body whose dreams are worthy of our attention and accomplishment. It is our honor to give them permission to do what God has put in their hearts and create a huge safety net for them to fall into as they step out into what God has made them for.

Many leaders might feel threatened when other amazing people start to emerge around them. However, what I have found in my own life is when I allow them to emerge, I experience the freedom that comes from trusting God with my calling and releasing others into their callings. Any other way makes us into a Saul, trying to destroy the Davids in our life that God Himself has appointed to bring forth His purposes on earth.

True fathers and leaders in the faith must understand their own identity and security before they're able to give the ministry away. As we all know, you can only lead someone as far as you have gone. God desires that our heartbeat would be to see His sons and daughters around us take hold of everything He ordained for their lives. God made champions to step into their destinies unhindered and encouraged to run the race set before them. In the words of John, "I have no greater joy than this, to hear of my children walking in the truth." A father's greatest joy is to see his children know the truth of who God made them to be and to live like champions in Christ Jesus.

Feeling threatened by someone else's greatness in God absolutely sucks. I have experienced this imprisonment firsthand, especially in the early years of Isla Vista Church. In those days our family lacked identity and safety, allowing a culture of comparison to form that enabled the seed of jealousy to grow in our family. Starting in 2007, God stripped our fellowship down to a core group of fifteen people, which allowed Holy Spirit to heal our hearts and rid our family of jealousy. I can honestly say I feel completely free in this area today because God has given Holly and I covenantal friends and co-laborers for the city of Isla Vista. I have been in awe watching God raise up a raw team of people who love Christ, one another, and His mission in the earth.

Leaders both create and shape the culture of a church family. If the leaders don't understand covenant they will never create a culture of champions. Champions are made in environments where trust is high and vulnerability is normal. I am not saying I have arrived, but I have tasted the fruit of covenant.

Covenant creates a safe place for the family to partner in order to see the dreams of heaven become a reality on earth. As the saying goes, "Team work makes the dream work." In my opinion, the days of the "Superstar" pastors will no longer define the church. The days ahead will be marked by many lovers of Jesus who are empowered by the Spirit and encouraged by the family to be God's champions for their families, friends, and places of influence.

WE ARE THE DREAMERS

MAC MONTGOMERY

Fostering Champions, Chostering Fampions. I don't know, you tell me. I've never been one to excel in academics. I'll tell you one thing I do know: I am a champ, and I have been fostered by other champs! Those champions have changed my life forever. I have learned what family was through them. I learned what heaven was through them. These people, specifically speaking, the Lomelinos and the family they've created in Isla Vista, have single-handedly changed my life just by letting me witness their obedience to the voice of the Lord. This family showed me what it meant to be citizens of heaven living out their citizenship here on earth.

These people showed me what it was like to be believed in. I had never experienced that before. Sure I had some friends, I had some mentors to look up to, but I was never the top achiever or anything. There weren't a lot of situations where people were congratulating me for doing something awesome. I was the kid growing up who had only a couple of friends. I kept to myself a lot. I was constantly drawing and sketching on my schoolwork, never engaging in the class or the teacher, just lost in my own little world of creativity. I was the kid who was petrified of "pop-corn" reading. I was terrified of being called on in front of the class. I would rather just draw something and think of how much cooler that was than the book we were reading.

Needless to say, I felt very misunderstood from a young age. This pattern followed me through high school. People just thought I was a slacker. I wasn't. I was never a slacker. I just operated differently than most of the world. Since nobody knew what to do with me, I was always considered a lazy student or a nobody who wouldn't amount to much. Though I didn't excel in school, I would go home after school and play my guitar for hours. I would draw and make sketches like nobody's business! I could memorize entire movies after watching it one time. My mom always said, "If only you could memorize your school-work the way you can memorize movies! You could be the smartest man ever!" She knew I was smart, but she thought that it would look different. I was already very smart; it just wasn't shown through the schooling system. I have a great mom and a great dad, both of whom are very artistic in their own ways, but I would be as bold to say that they never fully under-stood me. They have been there for me, yet always wondering why I am the way I am.

So high school went by, one year of college went by, and finally I realized that I was not cut out for school. There is absolutely nothing wrong with the schooling system by any means. I have always been very different, cut from a different cloth. So 2009 rolled around, and I had been leading worship at dif-ferent things around Santa Barbara for about three years. I had somewhat of a reputation for being some-one to lead worship and the presence of God show-ing up—nothing huge, just another anointed worship leader in Santa Barbara.

One night, I was leading worship at something called Glory Night in Santa Barbara. This was the summer after my first year of Bible College, and I knew God was calling me to Isla Vista, I just didn't know how I would get there or with what group. I knew Jason Lomelino, the Senior Pastor at Isla Vista Church, from doing Jesus Burgers out in IV. He and I had had somewhat of a relationship before this night, but nothing too deep. It was simply that we had both shared a heart to see Isla Vista redeemed. But this one particular night after leading worship, Jason asked me to become the worship pastor at Isla Vista Church. I was nineteen years old, with one desire in life at that time: to see Isla Vista come to know the love of Jesus. So of course I said yes! It was as if God had come down from Heaven, and given me this invitation to be a part of a massive revival that will impact the world forever! It was from then on that God brought me on this long journey of entering into family and understanding covenantal relationship.

I had never been a part of a real functioning family. As I said, my parents were great, but it wasn't an ideal situation for a kid to grow up in. I had yet to see what a family looked like that was healthy and functioning in love and peace amongst one another. This was where I found all that. Right here, in one of the craziest party cities in the world, I found family.

As I mentioned before, growing up in school was an interesting experience to say the least. But moving into Isla Vista and being fathered and mothered by Jason and Holly was like nothing I had ever experienced! I had never heard anyone say, "We believe in you!" or, "Dream big and go after it. We are all for you!" It was crazy! These people really did believe in me. I will never forget the first time I actually understood that.

One night after church, we were all hanging out

in the Lomelinos' living room, and I was having a hard time believing in my identity. I was struggling with all the lies that had been spoken over me my entire life. Nineteen years of believing I was not good enough and believing that nothing I did would ever amount to anything seemed to all add up in that moment. Someone asked me something, I don't even remember what, but I do remember that I tried so hard not to cry as I answered them. Everyone in the room suddenly directed their attention to our conversation, and I just lost it. I just started bawling about how I had never done anything and how I never would and that there was no fruit amounting to anything in my life. I was crying because I believed all the lies that the enemy had spoken over me. What happened next was something that I had never experienced before in my short life.

Everyone, I mean everyone, in that room stopped what they were doing and began to prophesy the Father's heart over me. Jason and Holly, and some others who were there, all laid their hands on me and began to pray over me and affirm me for the man I was. They declared that my life has produced a lot of fruit, and that their lives were some of the fruit of my love. I mean talk about my world getting absolutely rocked! I began to hear these people's thoughts about me, and they were thoughts I had never even come close to thinking about myself. But, the craziest part about it all was that those were God's thoughts being spoken over me. Everyone in the room that night was agreeing with God about my life and about who I truly was. I belonged! I was accepted! There was nothing weird about me! Sure I was a little different on some levels, but that is something God loves about me. He said, "That is how I made you! Learn who I am, in order to learn who you are, then, go and change the world with My love!"

We were a family, and I was loved and accepted not because of what I had ever done but because of who God said I was. They believed in me for who I was, not who I should or could be. They championed me. For the first time in my life, I fully believed that I would change the world. Everything was in seed form, but I knew that God would do something huge through me.

Since then, I have grown up into a man of God, fighting for those who aren't necessarily the first to be believed in. I have come out with two worship albums under the covering of Isla Vista Church, aka my family. God has put a vision and a dream in my heart to redefine the sound that people think they can encounter God to. In other words, being creative with writing worship music, not sounding like everyone else, and giving permission to the rest of the world to walk in their identities and make a sound that only they can make! God is a creator, and He made us to be creative too! I never knew why I was always drawing and playing music and not able to do well in school, but God knew. I didn't know who I was, but God did, and He surrounded me with a family of believers in Isla Vista who knew how to champion each other. They knew how to believe in me when I couldn't, and now I can believe in myself.

God has given me the ability to raise up a generation of worshipers who believe in themselves and know who they are in Christ. It is all about knowing what God thinks about you and that the finished work of Jesus on the cross was truly good enough to bring you into right standing and make you whole, pure, and clean before the Father. It took a family who knew that about themselves to take me in and tell me how amazing I was. Now I have received that revelation, believing that God thinks I am really something special, and that He has put a crazy anointing on my life! I am now able to do the same for others.

I have always been a champion—I just didn't know it. My family took care of me and reminded me what a champion I was, and now I am able to do that for others. YOU are a champion, and Jesus is madly in love with you. He has raised you up to change the world, one person at a time. Know you are loved, and you will be able to love the world and change it forever.

FROM DELINQUENCY

ERIK MASON

I'm not good with introductions (or conclusions for that matter), so I hope you don't mind if I jump straight in. I was raised in the wondrous state of Alaska in a partially Christian home. I make mention of my home being partially Christian because it was solely my mother who was a Christian in my youth; no one else in my family fully lived out our convictions until many years later. I also make mention of being raised in Alaska because I like to boast about Alaska—but that's beside the point. The point is that I was always, to some degree, around Christianity. From the age of five to perhaps twelve, I was inducted into a world of things that I did not fully understand. However, at age twelve, I had a revelation that God was quite real—not just a figure or idea—but an actuality. After this point, life suddenly made much more sense with its direction and purpose.

Consequently, I became much more aware of the details of life. In the following six to ten years after, there were victories and intimate moments with Jesus. But there was also an ongoing battle between me being a strong young leader in the Christian community and me being a godless, untrustworthy, delinquent rebel. This battle raged throughout my years in youth group, Bible college, and mission work in Central America.

As a result of this battle within me, I hurt many people along the way. During all those times of darkness and pain, I was involved in ministry. I've been involved in some sort of ministry since I was fourteen or fifteen years old. No matter how close to God I felt that I had gotten, or how long I went without doing something stupid or awful, I always felt these underlying thoughts that would sound something like, "Maybe I'm not good enough . . . maybe I should kill myself . . . maybe I should run away . . . everyone hates me . . . why do I hurt so bad . . . why don't you like me, God?" I promise this to you right now, if you have had thoughts like these, they are not true, and they are not to be held on to. They are not God's thoughts about you, and they don't have to be yours to own anymore.

In 2008, right before I went to Costa Rica to do mission work with a Christian missionary organization called SEND Ministries, a man named Jeshu, who was called a prophet (I now believe it as well), introduced me to the revelation that God didn't hate me, but rather loved me. That is a mere moment in a vast story, and all I can mention of it right now is that without that moment, I imagine I would have been lost in delinquency and self-loathing forever. Jeshu and Danny (the founder) and the rest of SEND, thank you forever.

In J. R. R. Tolkien's work *Lord of the Rings* the main protagonist, Frodo, reminisces about something that his older cousin Bilbo told him, "'It's a dangerous business, Frodo, going out of your door," he used to say. "You step into the Road, and if you don't keep your feet, there is no knowing where you might be swept off to'" (Bk. II, Ch. 3, Pg. 87). I feel fairly sympathetic to that. The last several years of my life have been "dangerous business": traveling to numerous places, seeing the world, vagabonding, and working in ministry, all the while feeling like my soul was in constant turmoil. Along the way, because of two unique and profound friendships of humble beginnings with Justin Huntsman and Mac Montgomery, I heard of and eventually visited Santa Barbara and Isla Vista Church. My first visit in 2009 was, to be brief, incredible. Santa Barbara became a place of rest and solitude, of spiritual refreshment. Eventually I moved to Santa Barbara; I guess you could say I moved there just to become part of the family.

The love of the family of IVC was, and is, life changing. The power and authenticity of the Spirit that IVC walks in is life giving. I had already believed in prophecy before my first visit there, but I was soon struck with how often, freely, and lovingly these people bestowed the thoughts and promises of God on each other. It seemed like all the time. No joke. These prayers were genuine, like between a child and father; sincere, like between intimate best friends; and conversational, like between two people instead of just one. Each of these prayers of prophecy for one another was soaked in love, carrying the heavy presence of power. I remember people gathering around me just to thank God for me. Or other times when I had a question in my head and someone would answer the question without me speaking it out loud. This deeply encouraged me to bring this ideal to every place I went. Prophecy played a big role in my own arrival into family.

There were people in my life who took continual steps of faith by involving their lives with mine, even when the majority of people saw me as someone not worth the risk. I can honestly attribute my metamorphosis in greatest density to two people: Danny Williamson and Jason Lomelino. These two men have both been integral in my life. I have many dear friends that must also be attributed with credit; I am not the work of anything less than a spiritual family who has loved me dearly.

I first met Danny in Germany during my fourth semester of Bible college. It was a fairly difficult semester for me since I was about to graduate with no clue of what I was going to do. Most of my friends had plans of some sort or had been asked to be interns or staff at one of the many campuses. Not me. I was convinced that the church wanted nothing to do with me. I felt like I was always fighting against some preconceived notion that I was a devious manipulator who was bound to err so fatally that there would never be forgiveness for my betrayal. I felt that way often, even with people I'm sure did not actually think that about me. Nevertheless, I had never once felt that with Danny.

From the first moment I met him, he saw something in me. Even when I felt like I, along with everyone else, saw nothing at all. I spent the next two and a half years being around Danny, and never once have I felt like he was unwilling to trust me, even though some of my actions would have proven to other people that I was untrustworthy. He found me as a hurting, bitter, negative delinquent, and he never failed to love and encourage me through every mistake.

I have known Jason for a few years now, but at the beginning our meetings and conversations were intermittent since I lived elsewhere and was consistently traveling. The condition of me feeling valued by Jason is not based upon the factor of me being magnificently or blatantly valuable. I would be sincerely shocked if I heard that there exists one person who did not feel valued by Jason. That seems like a boast and I'm well aware of this, because it is. I am not saying that Jason has never done anything wrong or had bad interactions, but Jason does have vivid love and genuine interest in people.

I moved up to Santa Barbara on a whim out of bad circumstances, nearly drowning in all the problems and hurt I had caused. I felt instantly cared for by Jason and the family of Isla Vista Church. It is truly inexplicable. I am unsure of what extent Jason was aware of my background, but it came with a warning. Regardless of what he did or did not know, it is still very odd for a pastor of a church to invest in someone that he does not know at all. However, the true magic of Jason's influence in my life happened in around thirty seconds, although the amount of time spent together is still growing exponentially. We were at a men's group and Jason said something that changed the very fabric of who I am. All he said was, "I see no guile in you." He was referencing John 1:47 where Jesus says to Nathanael that he is an Israelite in whom there is no guile (deceit). I cannot promise that these words will have the same effect in you, but it changed everything for me.

The thought of being trustworthy is different than the thought of being loved. Before that point in life, I was convinced that I would forever struggle against the deceitfulness in me that everyone seemed to see. All my life I had a dualistic conflict in the deepest part of me over being pure or being tainted, and for whatever reason people would only see the tainted part. When Jason said that, I wasn't even sure I could accept what he said because it was so what I desired to be and feel, but all these years it had seemed so distant and unattainable. And yet, the power of those words took their effect in those short few moments. I was trustworthy, able to do things well, and could be involved with people by investing in others without fear of hurt. I am not sure how the lie started or continued to build, or even how the processes and elements of such things all work together. I do know one thing for certain: if a person doesn't believe that they are capable of something, they never will be, they will never want to be, and they will never try to be.

Many people who don't know their calling to greatness are called to be great in and for the Kingdom of God. There are many champions of Jesus out there that have no idea of their destiny or how to walk in their calling. I was one of them. When a person feels called to be great for God but has no idea how to manage or steward that destiny in their lives, it can breed a dark and dubious nature within them. This in turn affects their interactions with people. They know they can do amazing things but are unable to accomplish them, either because of their fear of failure or because of sin's degrading effects on their lives. It can become a perpetual cycle in their interactions with the church. Because these Christians feel untrustworthy in their own heart, the church will treat them as untrustworthy. Thus, the church and its members may withhold their love and investments in fear that they will be squandered or taken advantage of.

Henri Nouwen once wrote, "Many ministers today are distant men who do not want to get their fingers burnt" (*Wounded Healer*). That is to say that the very basis of redemption is ransoming something, a payment for something; there is a sacrifice involved. It seems that people can forget that they may have to put their lives, with its various valuable components, at risk in order to save someone from the fire. The beauty of sacrifice is that it is not so concerned with the loss but focused on the gain.

I remember a conversation with a friend about his fear of his desire to be great for God ultimately disqualifying him from being great for God. It is sad to think that his God-given desire to do great things was in question. There are many champions amongst us, people who will make our Lord's name known and great in the nations. The problem is that when you look into the face of a delinquent, you can't easily see the heart of a champion behind the shroud of obstruction of what the world has made. Maybe it is safe to say that everyone is actually a champion, not a delinquent at all, if we would only take the time to see the champion within.

CALLED INTO A HIGHER PLACE

ALLIE MERRILL

The famous words of C. S. Lewis, little did I know at the time, defined the condition of my heart for a good eighteen years. He said, "If you want to make sure of keeping . . . [your heart] intact, you must give it to no one—not even an animal . . . lock it up safe in the casket or coffin of your selfishness. But in that casket . . . it will change . . . it will become impenetrable, irredeemable. To love at all is to be vulnerable." Unfortunately, I have related to that quote more times than I would like. I have lain there in that coffin allowing pain and loneliness in like a welcomed guest. At a time when it seemed that my heart was irreparable I began to let love in, and get out of the coffin. Only God knew it was the beginning of a new life filled with growth, family, encouragement, and love like I had never known.

I grew up with my older sister, younger brother, and parents in Carpinteria, California, a small town about thirty minutes south of Isla Vista. My family, I must say, is amazing. I have always had great relationships with each one of them, but even so, we have never been without our problems. Rehabs, hospitals, therapy sessions, and legal matters influenced most of my high school years. Looking back on that time, I was thrown back and forth as my body and mind were constantly manipulated by the drama. However, in the midst of it all, I remained in the coffin, numb and feeling nothing. Even being ignored by my friends became an all-too-familiar feeling for me. Yet somehow, God always had a way to penetrate the thick walls of my heart. My relationship with God teetered between two worlds: one, enduring the weight of unsolvable problems with my impenetrable heart; and the other, experiencing intimacy with my Father in Heaven and longing for so much more.

Growing up, the term "family" became a very individualistic term. A spirit of isolation rested in our home, participated in our conversations, and influenced each one of us. It was the norm in my family at that time, and no one knew better to raise their hand in petition. This bred strength in me to take on all the hardships alone, and it made me cling to the power of my hardened heart. My sister's frequent emotional ups and downs dragged me in and out of hospital doors and therapy rooms for years. It was all happening to us as a unit, but we were all experiencing it alone.

I remember one of the first times I experienced those hardships head on. I was shopping with my sister and her friend, when suddenly, I was being interrogated by the police while my sister was being handcuffed and taken to jail in the back of a police car. She was bawling, but I just stood there staring at her, confused and upset that she would steal eight hundred dollars worth of clothing right in front me while I had no idea it was happening. I later found out about other instances occurring before this that my parents had not told me about. In their defense, they were only trying to protect me, but it got to a point where they could keep only so much from me. My sister would lie to me and keep me in the dark about everything because she didn't want "her sins to smudge my white garments." That only made me feel more isolated and untrustworthy, so I chose to ignore everyone and everything that was going on. I began to "lock my heart up in a coffin" at this point and my heart grew harder and harder. Over time, she began to tell me more stories, and eventually it became so much that I didn't want to talk with her at all. The rest of my family didn't speak of those things either, unless we were forced to in a therapy session. I was accused of not loving my sister at all, but part of me didn't want to. The truth is, I didn't know how.

I felt love was a solid object I needed to reach for. It was never sappy or vulnerable, but always strong; and this was the role I began to take on. In one therapy session, I sat across from my sister as twenty plus people watched her cry her heart out expressing how much she loved me. I wanted so badly to respond in the same manner, but all I could do was sit there and stare at her with dry eyes and say, "I love you, too." I meant it, I really did, but the therapists muttered under their breath, "Well, isn't this interesting," as if I were a science experiment that didn't match their textbook answers. "Her face sure isn't backing up her words one bit." I knew they doubted my words, but I honestly didn't know how to show emotion. My heart made a home in that coffin and took all my emotions captive. I thought there was something severely wrong with me, or that maybe God gave me a plastic heart, afraid of feeling and unable to know love. Therapy sessions became a joke, hospital visits became less critical, and family interventions became less hopeful. I mastered how to curb every feeling that surfaced and put on as much strength as I could. As a result, I became the strong pillar of my family; a rock that never spoke from the heart.

As tragic events continued to eat away at my

family, God began revealing my need for healthy relationships over the course of seven months. I desperately needed a friend I could talk to apart from my mom and disinterested friends. God showed me that I didn't know how to love because I didn't know how to receive it. As unfamiliar as it sounded, the idea that weakness is actually strength challenged my heart to rest and receive. Isla Vista Church played a huge role in this.

After God opened up my eyes to my need for deep relationships, I spent a good three months crying out for a real family that I could be a part of. One Friday afternoon, God answered my prayers and told me to go to Jesus Burgers, so I grabbed a friend and we headed to IV. I walked into the prayer shed and immediately saw McEagan (Mac) Montgomery for the first time in about four years. We knew each other from high school and Calvary Chapel youth group, but hadn't kept in touch. We ended up sitting and talking through the night for what seemed like hours, and it became confirmed in my heart as he pressed me to become a part of IVC that I finally belonged somewhere—there, at that house, in that church, with those people, in that family. I was shocked how vulnerable I felt with them, and for the first time I was in a place that wouldn't ignore me. Their love for the people of IV and the way that everyone came around and befriended me without me having to do a thing was something I had never experienced before. The love was so genuine in every person, and I knew I needed to be a part of it.

I ended up moving into the Jesus Burgers house in June 2012 and began playing with the FMLYBND. Little did I know, the Lord wanted to tear down and build back up the meaning of family, of friendship, and of love in my life. By coming under certain people in Isla Vista Church, I re-learned friendship, trust, and honor. Mac and Braelyn Montgomery, Erik and Krissy Mason, and all the girls in the Jesus Burgers house played a huge role in this.

Two particular experiences with the family of IVC clearly depict how the family of God is supposed to function and champion one another into demolishers of the kingdom of darkness. I love these stories because they display exactly how the love of God works.

One Sunday, I tried to run home before worship because I felt the spirit of oppression that often comes over me. Mac grabbed me just before I headed out the gate and had everyone around pray and prophesy over me. I stood there refusing to receive and accept what was going on. That's when Erik said, "Allie, you really just need to receive this." Before all that happened, I tried to express my hatred for the situation to Mac in hopes of him letting me leave by saying, "I hate you right now." But it didn't seem to work because he just laughed, hugged me, and said, "That's okay, I love you, too."

My second story begins on the drive home from an IVC retreat with Erik and Krissy Mason. Erik was talking about family and carrying each other's burdens, but in my mind I thought, "Trust me, I won't be here in two weeks. It always happens that way." I'll never forget what he said in the car, "Allie, you're a part of this family now, whether you believe that or not. You can try and leave, but you will never not be a part of this family. Which means you can't just leave the room to deal with your problems alone anymore. Whatever you're going through, we're going through it with you."

Erik and Krissy decided to spiritually adopt me and cover me with Godly wisdom, advice, and most importantly, friendship. Together they are my coaches and my biggest fans. At times it is hard because my old thoughts tell me to run away and ignore the issues of my heart. But I am leaving those thoughts in the coffin. As they continue to pursue me relentlessly, I see the fruit in my own life of championing someone into a greater place. I feel believed in, and I feel loved.

Ever since I became a part of IVC, people have not stopped encouraging me. They haven't stopped praying for me, blessing me, receiving prophetic words for me, all for the purpose of loving me. There hasn't been a day that I have woken up in the Jesus Burgers house thinking, "I'm not loved here." It is actually quite the opposite. I have never had more of a desire to pursue my calling in worship music and a lifestyle of intimacy with God, and it is simply because I have an entire family pushing me forward. Much like what Mac did when I wanted to run away, the family grabs hold of me and makes sure my relationship with Christ is constantly growing. This is why Erik, like a spiritual dad and coach, was so adamant that I receive all that God was trying to say to me that day. That is the beauty of this family in Christ. Everyone is looking out for one another's relationships with God, because friendship with Him is the most sacred and important thing in this life.

Living in this environment involves walking into your house knowing you have six people ready and willing to pray for you in a heartbeat if needed. Krissy took me in the prayer house one day, sat with me, and walked me through how to prophesy. She put my hands on her and said, "Go—get a word for me." At first I laughed, but it is that kind of challenge that causes one to really practice the gifts of God. It is being able to trust and rely on a whole group of people for anything—spiritually, emotionally, or financially. This family has allowed me to grow in the things that God is calling me to without fear of failure, or fear of judgment. Krissy and Erik always tell me, "Allie, we will never be done with you. We don't have an agenda to fix you either. We're not your therapists. We're not your mentors. We're your friends, and we care that you know Jesus."

IVC doesn't have a handbook or a systematic equation on how to fix brokenness or lessen suffering. We simply believe in God's promise that "He will place the lonely in family." We also believe in lifting and championing one another in order for our relationships with God to have intense intimacy. When a person is offered and receives love, it catapults them into a deeper relationship with God. That is the desire of every person at IVC, and every person who truly loves Jesus. Love, love, love—that's what it's all about.

DESTINED FOR HIGH PLACES

MICHELLE QUEZADA

"O SHEPHERD. YOU SAID YOU WOULD MAKE MY FEET LIKE HINDS' FEET AND SET ME UPON HIGH PLACES."

HINDS' FEET ON HIGH PLACES
~HANNAH HURNARD

W ell,' he answered 'the only way to develop hinds' feet is to go by the paths which the hinds use.' " Like Much-Afraid, the main character in Hannah Hurnard's book *Hinds' Feet on High Places*, I was much-afraid of the journey God wanted to take me on. At an early age, God deposited an amazing amount of faith in me because He knew the path set before me would require every ounce of it. As a child, my experience in the Seventh-Day Adventist church was a list of rules that I couldn't keep and a lack of freedom that I didn't understand. Even in the midst of frustration and boredom, I still believed in God, but it wasn't enough to win me over.

As I entered my freshman year of high school, I was over people telling me how to live my life. I decided I was going to party and finally have the freedom I so longed for. Little did I know that I was enslaving myself in much more than I bargained for. During my freshman year, I met Hana, a fun and lively girl who loved Jesus. She invited me to her church's youth group, and I was blown away with how different everything was. I went on a mission trip to Mexico with the youth group, and it was then that I saw a glimpse of Jesus. I tried to keep the flame going, but like any spiritual high, it eventually burnt out. My sophomore and junior years are a blur due to the alcohol and drugs I consumed almost every weekend. In the midst of my hooking up with guys and partying, I still led worship at my youth group. Looking back at those years, I remember desperately wanting to escape it all and step into the depths of my real identity and inheritance. But, I was looking for acceptance and placing my worth in all the wrong places.

It was senior year of high school when I had to make a decision about the next step in my life. As I watched friends open their acceptance letters to colleges, I decided that I wanted more of a college experience than what I was going to get by staying at home. Since it was too late to apply to most universities, I started looking into community colleges in Southern California. Before I could have made up my mind, I felt like God started speaking to me about Santa Barbara. I knew it was God, but I chose to ignore it. Until one night when I was sitting in the hallway and asked God, "Hey, if you really want me to go to Santa Barbara, can you please make it obvious?" Then the next day a friend approached me at school and proceeded to inform me of her decision to decline her acceptance to Sonoma State University. She asked me, "Michelle, we should go to Santa Barbara City College! You down?" Without hesitation I shouted, "Yes!" It was at that moment that I knew whatever God had for me in Santa Barbara was going to be an adventure.

Four years later, and it has been the sweetest adventure yet. I got connected with Isla Vista Church through a friend from Cru, a campus ministry at University of California, Santa Barbara. IVC is more than a sit-in-the-back-row-and-slip-out-before-someone-comes-over-to-talk-to-you kind of church—it is family. It is a place where it is safe to be vulnerable and okay to mess up. So often we treat church like a fast-food restaurant, looking to get fed and completely missing the point of why God sets the lonely in families (Psalm 68:6).

I didn't know it at the time, but I was lonely. I knew all the right things to say that avoided breaking down the barricaded fortress I had built up around my heart. It was only a matter of time until God would tear down these walls, as He alone knows how to truly protect my heart.

I was created with a purpose to be a radically anointed worship leader. But I was not always this confident in my destiny. In fact, I ran away from every opportunity I had to really take on the calling over my life. For the most part, I did a really good job of hiding behind people, until I came into a family that saw the destiny over my life and wouldn't take no for an answer. I resisted, I cried, and then I resisted some more, as I was being thrust into all the things that scared me about being a worship leader. The big problem that kept me from this great destiny God had for me, on top of many other insecurities I was dealing with, was that I didn't believe in myself. Even though I had every prophetic confirmation and encouragement in my destiny, I just didn't believe it—any of it. I had faith in God but lacked faith in myself, which caused me to doubt the truth and believe the lies the enemy desperately wanted me to believe.

Mac Montgomery was a shaping force in me coming into my calling. You may know him as the worship pastor for IVC, or you may not know him at all, but I know him as the guy who single-handedly pushed my buttons in every way imaginable. While pushing my buttons, he pushed me into the destiny he knew God had for me. He saw the destiny over me and always did a good job reminding me of it—even if it meant dragging me to the places I was scared to go on my own.

At one Sunday gathering, Mac asked me to lead worship (more like told me I was, and I had to be okay with it, out of love of course). Instead I asked someone else to play for me because I didn't get my shift covered at work, but mostly because I was afraid to do it. I strolled into church, well into Jason's sermon, assuring myself that Mac would not get mad at me for not leading because I had a valid excuse. That day I saw that my actions really do have consequences. What I choose to run away from will hurt all those who are choosing to stand and fight for me. As I sat with Mac trying to defend myself he looked at me and said, "I'm not mad that you didn't lead a worship set today; I'm mad because you don't see that you are so capable and ready to do this." He hugged me as tears streamed down my face, and he told me he loved me and believed in me. It was in that moment that all the lies I had been believing were brought to the light and my fears of inadequacy were overcome by love. This family believed in me when I didn't, and they extended their hand to pull me up to higher places than I could have ever reached on my own or even had the guts to climb.

Even while I was leading worship in high school and still dabbling in the party scene, God had a plan for me. Carlos Devitis, my high school youth pastor, was one who stood by me and let me discover the path that my Shepherd had for me. As we were catching up one day, he told me that he knew I was partying the whole time I led the youth worship team. Shocked and a little embarrassed, I asked him why he allowed me to continue playing. Pointing at the exit, he explained, "Because God said that the minute you felt judged you wouldn't hesitate to walk through that door and into the door of another party." Carlos trusted God's voice and chose to walk alongside me and believe in the destiny over my life rather than allow fear to throw me back into the world where my dreams would never be fostered.

Honestly, I don't know where I would be without family. I have cried in many arms, leaned on many shoulders, and shared many smiles and laughs with these people. Church is more than numbers, it is more than a well-known pastor, and it is even more than how good the sermon was that day. Church is all about family—opening up to people and taking the risk to live transparently before them. Everyone is longing to be accepted, and everyone is looking to love and to be loved in return. Well, look no further because God wants to set your eager heart in a family that is ready to love you and lift you up to your destiny at any cost.

REDEFINING PERFECT

JESSICA BRAZIEL

I remember sitting in a pew in a Southern Baptist Church when I was five years old saying the prayer that forever changed my life. I accepted Christ as my Savior that day and have been on a journey ever since. Because, you see, speaking that prayer is just the beginning of a splendid adventure with God for eternity.

I was raised in a close-knit family by two compassionate parents and three built-in best friends, or as most call them, sisters. And I have always felt the pressure to be perfect. This pressure, more often than not, was something I placed on myself. I wanted to be accepted and to live up to expectations that I thought others placed on me, even if they pushed me to be someone different than who I was or who God created me to be. There was a pressure to be the perfect Christian, perfect friend, perfect student, and perfect daughter who always followed the rules. Everything I did had to be perfect, and a fear of failure always followed right behind me, waiting to take hold of me at any second.

When I was twelve years old, my eldest sister had a baby and our family dynamics completely changed.

Now instead of pressuring myself to be perfect to fit in with others, I felt I had to be perfect to gain my father's approval and attention. No matter what I did though—straight As, getting on the club soccer team, or winning triple jump league champion for track—it never seemed to be enough. This is when I began to compartmentalize my feelings. I was constantly at a masquerade ball changing masks with each group of people I was surrounded by. I never allowed myself to be vulnerable, and always lived with walls up. On the rare chance that I honestly told someone how I felt, they seemed not to care, and I would regret ever trusting them. My prayer journal became the only one who ever knew exactly how I felt.

During this time, I was still in love with God and had a relationship with Him, yet I knew something was missing. I believed the lies that I was unworthy, unloved, and imperfect, and because of these lies, I didn't feel like I deserved to have friends or build relationships with people. Sadly, when I transferred to UCSB, I still longed to be accepted by those around me and willingly molded myself to be who I thought they expected me to be. It worked for a little while, but God was doing something in my heart that eventually caused me to put an end to the masquerade.

I began to get tired of not having people really know me, and I longed for a home church and a family-like community that loved me for who I was—sans mask. God was faithful, and I met a girl from Isla Vista Church in UCSB's Carrillo Dining Commons one day at dinner. She invited me to come to church that Sunday, and the best part was that IV Church was close enough for me to walk to. At church that afternoon, Pastor Jason welcomed me personally, and it was the first time that I felt like I was coming to spend time with family instead of just coming to a building. This was exactly what my heart was longing for, and it was at that moment that I knew I was home. At the end of service, Jason called for a time to pray and prophesy over one another. Brittany, the friend who invited me, shared with me the picture that God gave her for my next season. Immediately I felt God's love for me pumping through my veins. Overwhelmed by the enormity of His love, I started crying. God began to speak to me about why He loved me and how valued I was. I felt like I was enveloped in this love cloud and God was giving me a hug. For the first time, I felt like it was okay to not be perfect, because God loved me in spite of my actions. He loved me simply for being me.

God was no longer someone who loved me from afar, but rather a best friend I wanted to spend all my time with. I found myself reading my Bible to learn more about Him and what He thought of me, rather than because I felt it was a requirement. I knew that it was time to let down my walls and build relationships with people, but I didn't want to be transparent with just anyone. God showed me how well He knew me, and encouraged me to take a leap of faith, by bringing key people from the IV Church family into my life. While it was hard to be open with people before, these people provided a safe place for me to be vulnerable.

Isla Vista Church opened up a place for me to live in freedom to be who God created me to be. They encouraged me to always put what God said about me before what others said. They taught me to spend time reading my Bible in order to hear the promises God had for me. And they also provided me with a freedom to fail, which I am still coming to understand.

I learned about many new and different facets of the faith, such as tongues, prophecy, and healing, through relationship with the Holy Spirit. God blessed me by calling me to grow in each of them, but

I struggled with learning how to be perfect at them. Fortunately, I had a family surrounding me, letting me know there was no perfect way; it is all through love and being led by the Holy Spirit.

While I was learning how prophecy ties into daily life with God, He placed me in a home group where we read a book about all the different ways He speaks to His kids. It was a safe place to practice prophecy on my family with the freedom to fail. I learned that God spoke to me differently than anyone else in the group, and there was no way to fail in hearing from God. Prophetic words do not have to be earth shattering; they can be a simple feeling or a picture. It was all amazing!

Through the encouragement and love of the IV Church and my family—even when things made no sense—I continued to step out in faith when God called me to do something. I loved Him, and I wanted to love other people so they would experience the love God had for them. Every Friday night, I would go to Jesus Burgers and prepare the buns with condiments at the barbecue, and every time my heart came alive as I got to love the people of Isla Vista.

In the back of my mind I knew God was calling me to go practice my prophetic gifting in a new environment, to take that leap of faith and love people well. He showed me that because I receive prophetic words different than I thought I would, I was fearful of giving a wrong word. It was a battle for me to work my way across the street to the spiritual encounter sign, the sign that marks where we love the people of Isla Vista through prophecy and healing. It was a big step that required me to be vulnerable and willing to fail because I might pray for healing and not see results immediately, and that people might laugh because they thought we were silly.

After a few weeks of God encouraging me to

prophesy, I took a baby-step of faith and moved to the fire pit. God brought people to me who needed to hear how much God loved them and who He called them to be. Just as family encouraged me in my identity, so I wanted to do the same for others. Every Friday night, God would give me insight into different people's personality, their dreams, and what He loved about them. As I grew in boldness and shared what He told me, I was happily surprised with their responses: they felt loved and known by God. For those specific people, it clicked that God was fully present and 100 percent interested in their lives. Seeing the accuracy and positive response of my words gave me more confidence to share what I received. I finally took the plunge and went across the street.

Loving people at the sign was scary at first, but I knew my IVC family was with me. We met hundreds of people at the sign and saw God do crazy things: broken bones were healed, legs grew out, sickness was no more, and people's identities were revealed. The greatest part of being at the sign was seeing people realize that God loved them just as they were! Seeing people encounter God in a real and tangible way made risking failure worth it.

Even though I am still a perfectionist, I am learning that it is okay to fail. I am more willing to be vulnerable and share what God has done in my life with strangers. I realize now that if I had never risked my comfort, people would not have encountered God. Without my family at IV Church encouraging me to step into my identity as God's beloved daughter, hundreds of people would not have experienced the God who loves unconditionally. Being able to love Isla Vista because others first loved me is the best part about being a member of the Isla Vista family!

HIS SUCCESS IS MY SUCCESS

AVA AMES

If there is one thing I have learned about walking with the Lord, it is that everyone is a work in progress. No one has reached any sort of finish line or exhausted all there is to learn from God; rather, we are all on a journey where we are constantly being refined in every area of our lives. Throughout my own journey, I have experienced freedom in knowing that God's unconditional love is endless and His infinite teachings are coated in patience and grace. This freeing love motivates me to face fears as He calls me to become more like Him every day. Having the family of God beside me throughout this process has helped bring forth the ultimate truth that my success and identity are hidden in Christ alone.

For most of my life, I have avoided confronting certain emotions. Only recently has God given me the love and strength to confront the fears that have held me back from experiencing the fullness of life. If God had not knocked on the door of my heart, uncovering the fear that resided there, I would have avoided facing my fears of trust and vulnerability for as long as possible. But thankfully, God is never threatened, overwhelmed, or angered by the mess in our lives. God is for us. We are sons and daughters of the King

(John 1:12–13), and our freedom lies in knowing that we are already successful because of Christ's redemptive work on the cross as an all-sufficient sacrifice. He truly is our ultimate champion. As children of God, our destiny is to live in freedom from the chains that once bound us, to be an expression of His love on earth, and to carry the joy of the Lord as our strength. In essence, we too are all called to be champions.

Before growing my relationship with Christ, my view of being a champion was entirely contingent upon my definition of success. I perceived success as something to be achieved after conquering a challenge, and only once conquered could I then be a champion. I was determined to be successful in whatever I put my mind to because, at the time, that was all I had been taught. I measured my success by how much I could accomplish independently and to what extent I could excel in family, academic, and personal spheres. I was convinced that this success would eventually steer me toward true fulfillment.

The majority of my fears regarding trust and vulnerability stemmed from growing up in a household where success was measured by worldly standards. My parents' perception of success placed business above family and work above relationships. Together, they indeed attained success as they became wealthy, traveled the world, and pursued their business endeavors for many years. After their divorce, I found myself increasingly wounded by the concept of family. My brother and I were often left feeling abandoned as nannies and relatives raised us while our parents pursued their careers. I learned to be self-sufficient since I couldn't depend on others to be there for me.

During this period I disregarded my emotional wellbeing and would instead distract myself with goals and aspirations. In other words, I strived to create the external appearance of perfection. Over time, I began to notice that even though my family was prosperous by the world's standards, my home felt empty and my heart despondent. Throughout my life when I'd encounter disappointment, I coped by becoming desensitized to problems and feigning strength. To me, weakness meant giving in to my emotions through allowing the pain to surface. Even crying about what I was feeling seemed pathetic and pointless.

By the time I entered college, I was ready to leave home—not simply to start a new chapter, but to start an entirely new book. I desperately wanted my future to be different from my past, but I still lived in the fear that I was bound to repeat my family's mistakes and tendencies. As I continued to preoccupy myself with school and my social life during college, I began to notice that the allure of goals and aspirations was no longer able to distract me from the emptiness I truly felt. Against such a façade of success, I failed miserably; I didn't feel accomplished, regardless of how much I did. Life seemed meaningless, and I couldn't shake a deceptive voice I constantly heard in my head, accusing me of being worthless. I was unfulfilled with all the world had to offer, I was hurt by the lies of my past, and I was disappointed with my inability to let go of it and believe in a better story.

During this time I became increasingly aware that I needed help. Whether or not God was real, I felt He was too far removed or preoccupied to have any relevance in my life. I did not believe that He had the desire or power to transform my life with His love. Growing up, I often saw people go to church on Sundays, listen to the sermon, and leave without even bothering to talk to anyone. Based on what I had observed, I assumed that committing to God was an internal promise, usually carried out on an individual basis. Even though I had attended church for many years, the importance of community was rarely emphasized. Based on my experiences, going to a Bible study once a week or having a discussion over a cup of coffee was my view of a Christian lifestyle. But the more I thirsted for fulfillment and thought about what it truly meant to be successful, the clearer the prominence of God became.

One Sunday, I ended up at IVC sitting in a pew and listening to the worship music when God fell afresh on me. All of my thoughts collided into a moment of pure clarity as I encountered the love of God pour over me. In that moment, I recognized that Christ is the ultimate champion through what He accomplished on the cross, having nothing to do with what I have or ever will accomplish. Everything in me knew that He was the only way, and my only hope. From that day forward, I willingly gave up my life to God.

God placed me in the IVC family after I committed my life to Him because He knew, far more than I did, that I needed loving, family-oriented relationships that this group effortlessly offered. It was through this family that God challenged my previous notions of church community and called me to invite others in on my walk with Him. God's love, as exhibited through the IVC community, began to renew my mind and shift the way I perceived the world. My entire life was being fully transformed as I was becoming a new creation in Him. I began to recognize success in a way that I had never fathomed before; I was living in the new covenant and clothed in Christ's success. I started treasuring relationships simply founded on love in my life. My relationship with God, family, and friends each adopted a new sense of worth that felt right and meaningful.

IVC became a safe place for me to learn how to practice being vulnerable with people who genuinely cared for me. The friendships that God placed in my life consistently served to complement the lessons that God was teaching my heart about my identity and success in Him. It was through these relationships that God revealed the importance of transparency and the freeing power of vulnerability in my life. These instrumental shifts happened in me when I said yes to God and decided to allow people to come alongside me. This took time and trust, but resulted in growth.

At first, it was strange to meet people my age that radically loved God and even stranger that they sincerely cared about my wellbeing. This was a new way of life that I had never experienced. Admittedly, the way these college students effortlessly exhibited love and kindness toward one another came across as unreal. But the more I stuck around and grew friendships with these people, the more convinced I became that they were just genuine lovers of Jesus who wanted to demonstrate the love they found in Him to others. Having people around me who passionately pursued the love of God made my journey with God not only stronger but also easier. I was able to confront fears in my life knowing that I had supportive friends around me who could be Christ to me if I became discouraged.

God journeyed even deeper with me as He desired to redeem my view of family and marriage. Thankfully, pastor Jason and his wife, Holly, became parents to me in ways that my real parents never were. They became my spiritual parents who brought me hope and encouragement. It took me time to realize how truly safe, loved, and secure being around them made me feel. It was Christ through them that served to foster my identity as a champion in Him. God has used their realness, honesty, and love to redeem my once cynical view of marriage and family. They both lovingly listen and freely offer their wisdom to me anytime in hope that I will learn from their mistakes and gain from their understanding. It is plain to see that their humble home is filled with wholeness, as people are met with love every time they walk through the door.

Jason and Holly's simple lives constitute testaments that success is birthed in relationship with God and cannot be bought or worked for; it simply exists through Christ's merit. Understanding that I am a daughter of God and receiving His love quenched my thirst for purpose and gave me identity and peace that I previously had not found in the world. For once in my life, I felt complete. My new family within IVC empowered and encouraged me throughout the ups and downs of life that previously left me feeling hopeless. The more time I spent with God and family, the more I began to develop fulfillment and joy that left me with the desire to share this love with others.

Again, while the success that Christ has accomplished in me is finished, I am a work in progress, continually growing in reverence of God's transformative love and its power to change people's lives through revealing true championship. The family that God gave me through IVC showed me that people are capable of being the expression of Jesus' love to others, and their lives bear the fruit of success simply through Christ living in them. My identity as a champion was nurtured through this family. And now, I am no longer living in the fear of failure or abandonment. Success has adopted a new meaning, which has left me fulfilled and hopeful. I now know that through building up family, we build up truth, and the truth is that we are already successful because of what Christ has accomplished for us on the cross—He is our ultimate champion.

Conclusion

Lucas Bell

Independently, we cannot attain the fullness of what God has for us, because He designed us with the need for each other. Fostering champions includes the practice of strong faith and belief in one another. When we choose to invest our lives into one another, champions are created. Our identity and anointings are hidden in Christ; family serves to bring forth these powerful truths. In a culture centered on the family of God, your success is my success. When a person steps into their anointing, everyone benefits. God designed family to empower the seeds of our destiny that He placed within each of us. To our joy, we celebrate the champion that each of us is becoming.

Family is simply an invested group of believing people. It constantly has our best interest in mind, and is committed to pursuing the fullness of God's plans for our lives. Similar to family in the natural, spiritual family is supportive of our success. To the extent that spiritual family fosters us into our identity as a champion of Him, we will be able to live in the fullness of our God-given destiny.

As Christ has already put His people at the right hand of the Father, our lives are about empowering each other to realize who we are in God and what He has made us for. Our greatness in God is founded in

Christ, empowered by the Holy Spirit, and encouraged by the church body through love. Pure, unconditional love fosters champions, as it "bears up anything and everything that comes" (1 Corinthians 13:7). This love empowers a community to behold themselves in God. Love nurtures any champion, regardless of their condition, as it reveals God's heart and releases them into their identity.

God creates His children to manifest His greatness. He gives us a family to nurture us into that greatness. As the church pushes God's children into their destinies in Christ, we form a family of powerful sons and daughters. Our lives are valuable and significant because He has covered us with the anointing of Christ. We must recognize that individual members cannot reach their full potential alone.

Spiritual fathers, mothers, brothers, and sisters believe in one another in both word and deed. When we foster champions, we demonstrate God's power of belief toward one another. The world has yet to know what we, as the body of Christ, can accomplish when we truly begin to believe in each other. The power of faith in one another will create a generation that is committed to each other's success.

The role of family changes the trajectory of lives. God puts us in relationship with one another to bring forth refinement and renewal in our identities in Him. For the children of God, fostering empowers us to mature into our positions as co-heirs in Christ. We must come to value the placement of those in our lives, as God is using these people to foster us. We will not become champions until we learn that we are all champions in His eyes and model a lifestyle that daily reflects this reality.

Our hearts long for people to believe in us and to care about our success; we need a family of people that will bear witness to our dreams unfolding. At

IVC, Mac has risen as an anointed worship leader because a family of people believed in him and provided a safe place for his destiny to be championed. It valued and accepted who God said he was, while caring for him. Now, he is pioneering a worship movement in which the presence of God is tangibly showing up, and championing others in their destiny.

Without a person like Mac speaking into her life, Michelle may have not come to realize that God created her to be a radically anointed worship leader. Mac taught Michelle not only to believe but also to be confident in her destiny. Mac became a voice of love speaking into Michelle's life. She could not excuse herself from God's plan for her life because people of faith surrounded her. Family lifts us up into our destiny even when we want to hide, and family is the daily reminder that we are no longer bound by fear. We are alive to God and His destiny for us.

The family is responsible for releasing the heart of God over us, breaking off lies of false identities, and discovering the hearts of champions. Erik grew up believing he was a tainted delinquent and not worth the risk. But His spiritual brothers and sisters treated him in a manner that directly countered these lies. Through word and deed, the family showed Erik the greatness God created him for. Currently, Erik pastors a Friday night gathering called the Upper Room and is growing as a gifted leader of God. Erik is one of many champions that needed a family to love him into his destiny.

To be championed in God is to be loved. The family of God is the direct manifestation of His love for people. We are the tangible expression of God to each other, a friendly invitation that God wants us to be together. Allie longed for a community that loved and encouraged her on a regular basis. God met her desire as He placed her in a spiritual family. The love she experienced in family broke her free from isolation and independence. Her church family provided an environment for her to grow in the promises of God over her life. They committed to her, even when she wanted to run. Members of a loving family devote themselves to each other, even when circumstances make this difficult; they do not give up on each other. In the midst of rejection, they respond with love and acceptance. Through the devotion of a committed family, love breaks down the walls of isolation and independence.

As we devote ourselves not only to each other's lives but also to each other's successes, we create a safe place for people to experience the depth of a family's commitment. Here, there is freedom to step out in faith and discover what God is calling each person to do. Jessica longed to be empowered to love others well. Family provided a safe place for her to take risks. It was not long until family and strangers alike were encountering God and His love through her. Because she experienced His love in a committed, safe environment, she was able to freely love others. In this security, children of God are empowered to love unconditionally through the power of the Holy Spirit.

Champions of God are successful in Him. In a culture of family, everyone is viewed as successful in Christ. Yet it takes each other to redefine our understanding of our position in Christ. The world creates false mentalities, which continually remind us to strive for our own individual success. But in family, we are capable of disarming these tendencies. Ava discovered the freedom of being vulnerable in the midst of a loving spiritual family; she found her identity as a child of God. While Ava felt safe and cared for, she began to understand true success: a relationship with God centered on love. Her success is now based on who she is in God, not on what she can achieve on her own merit. The nurturing care of family grew her identity in a safe environment, and now she walks through life as a champion of God.

Fostering champions is a royal privilege of the family of God. It is our birthright to hold each other accountable to the destiny that God has for our lives. Many have spent their entire lives longing to be in relationship with people who truly believe in them. God allows for this need, and then places us in family. Here, we belong to a community that believes in each other the way He does. The power of this belief holds us accountable to our potential and abilities in God. Fostering empowers the champion of God that we all are, as love "is ever ready to believe the best of every person" (1 Corinthians 13:7).

EPILOGUE

Family is the rhythm of God's heart, the manifestation of His relational intentionality, and the daily expression of the Kingdom in our lives. Through these stories, we see that God is faithful to place the lonely in family. His inclusive heart desires that we share life together as we become family.

Experiencing life together causes the Word of God to come alive, as His Spirit is constantly moving in our midst. As the life of God flows into our communities, we are ultimately creating a family of unconditional love. This love brings new paradigms of commitment, safety, and security to our hearts, as we build family on the model of heaven's unconditional love, not man's conditional love.

People are drawn into the family by the love of God manifesting in our midst. For most, family is an answer to the heart's eternal cry—we were made for each other. God fills our deep need for life-giving community with the unconditional love of the family. In the divine plan, God saw fit to shape entire communities around the image of His Son. As Jesus fulfills our need to be in relationship with the Father, family enables us to have relationship with our fellow brothers and sisters. As the people of God choose to live as family, we will be known for our love for one another.

He places us in community to grow us as a family

through the relationships we build. IVC has become a family through forming covenantal relationships amongst one another. In a covenantal community, we are committed to each other. Although this may look different for each relationship, there is a deep sense that our spiritual fathers, mothers, brothers, and sisters genuinely care about our wellbeing and are devoted to the work of God in our lives. As a family, this journey has not always been easy, but covenant has shown us the value of commitment, safety, and security.

Relationships such as these do not form overnight, but are fashioned through the journey of experiencing life with one another. Within these relationships we are given the permission to serve, encourage, and love one another. They place a high value on God's eternal purpose of family while enjoying Him and each other.

The growth from a church into a family has made fathering and mothering, community living, bonding through battle, and fostering champions possible. These core values are changing lives because they have been founded on the love of God and carried out through covenant. It is evident that the Holy Spirit has created many magnificent stories through the lives of these twenty individuals. Their stories inspire us to pursue a family movement, which God is steadily growing in this generation. The Father is passionate about His children doing life together, as this grows the culture of family.

Jesus has made a way for us to be in relationship with our Father and one another; He has released a new covenant of love. Isolation, independence, and loneliness no longer have the power to reign over our lives. We will see their influence lessen as we commit ourselves to each other. In the safety of family, we reform and rebuild our relational mindsets. This experience is not only valuable for the church today, but will serve to empower the people of God to transform the world. Our relational tendencies affect every area of our lives, as our beliefs about ourselves and others shape our representation of the Gospel in our daily lives.

We are intended to be the living representation of the Gospel to the world. In order for us to mature as sons and daughters of God, we need family to nurture us into our God-given identities and destinies. As church becomes family, we will be empowered and equipped to release the transformative power of Jesus in order for the Kingdom of Heaven to be established on the Earth.

ABOUT US

Isla Vista Church is a family of believers who desire to transform the city of Isla Vista and influence the nations with the good news of Jesus Christ. As we have pursued our city with the love of God, the Father has grown us into a family.

Our prayer through this book is for you, the reader, to embrace God's heart for raising covenantal communities that transform cities. We are all in the process of discovering the glorious expression of the church. We hope our stories inspire you to pursue Jesus and one another more, in addition to the call that God has on your church body. For some, this book may challenge you to rethink the way we "go to church" and practice our faith. For others, it may strengthen the good work that God is already doing.

The Isla Vista Church family is available in any way to help support the work of God in your community. Please contact us for more information. We also welcome you to visit our city and our family. We would love to hear about your own stories and testimonies of God's work in your city.

We invite you to visit our websites:

http://jesuslovesiv.com
http://islavistachurch.com

And to download our free iPhone and Android app search "Jesus Loves IV" in the app stores. Through this app you will be able to view our videos, which capture the life of our family transforming a city through the love of God.

Thank you for taking the time to read this book and hear our stories.

Bless you!
The Isla Vista Church Family

> *"DECLARE HIS GLORY AMONG THE NATIONS, HIS
> MARVELOUS DEEDS AMONG ALL PEOPLES. FOR GREAT
> IS THE LORD AND MOST WORTHY OF PRAISE . . .
> ASCRIBE TO THE LORD, ALL YOU FAMILIES OF NATIONS,
> ASCRIBE TO THE LORD GLORY AND STRENGTH. ASCRIBE
> TO THE LORD THE GLORY DUE HIS NAME."*
>
> *PSALM 96:3,7-8*

ACKNOWLEDGMENTS

Thank you, Father, for showing me what unconditional love and acceptance looks like in Christ. You alone have given me the greatest value for family and reaching a generation with the goodness of Your Son.

Thank you, Holly, for being my best friend and a wife whose worth is far above jewels. This journey we are on together of raising a family, both in the natural and spiritual is more than we could ask for or imagine.

To my four children and, Lord willing, my unborn children who will read this book one day, each of you have pulled the love of the Father out of me in more ways than you know. Endless books could never teach me what each of you have about what it means to be a dad. Thank you for all the sacrifices you have made over the years in sharing mom and me with so many people.

To the IV Church family, there are no other people I know who love God and one another the way you do; like I often say, "All fruit is family fruit."

To my parents, Holly's parents, brother in-laws, and sisters, thank you for the simple and extravagant ways you have shown love to our family over the years. Your love never goes unnoticed.

To Erik Krueger, Dan Hodgson, Bart Tarman, and Momma Bunny Koppa, thank you for pouring hours of truth and love into my life. I couldn't have asked for better mentors and spiritual parents for the different seasons of life I found myself in.

To Jacob Reeve, thank you for being such a good friend and brother. Thank you for your love for Isla Vista and all your years of labor here. Your love and suppport of the IVC family has been incredible.

Lastly, thank you to all who have supported the IV Church family and my family over the years. This book would not have been possible without your faithfulness both prayerfully and financially.

In Christ,
Jason Lomelino

Thank you, God, for being the best Dad! You always have more for your children.

To my Mama, thank you for empowering me to pursue my dreams.

To my Papa, thank you for giving me a sense of eternal value for this life and the one to come.

To Jason Lomelino, for carrying the love of God with your life. It's an honor to be your friend and brother.

To Jacob Reeve, your life has been one of my great teachers.

To Fred and Wendy Fereday, thank you for adopting me and releasing your good will into my life.

To Tucker Larson, you are one of the more intimate brothers in life.

To Justin Huntsman, you are a dear brother in the faith. Your life inspires the world to know Jesus.

To the IV Church Family, your lives wrote this book. Thank you for your hunger to know God and each other.

To our family editors, Tarra Rarick, Annalisa Morris, Ava Ames, Holly Lomelino, your time and skill have made this book beautiful. Thank you!

To all those who are seeking a deeper expression of community, may God lead you to your heart's desire.

Grace to you,
Lucas Bell

ALSO AVAILABLE

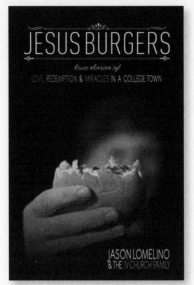

Jesus Burgers has remained the same since 2001 when a small group of beleivers grilled, flipped, and served the ministry's first burger, with a ketchup heart and a mustard cross.

The story of Jesus Burgers is told through the stories of over twenty people whose lives were transformed through this ministry in Isla Vista, California, an infamous party town adjacent to the University of California, Santa Barbara.

Sharing the love and hope of Jesus through a simple hamburger is what Jesus Burgers is all about. Isla Vista Church, a family of believers (mostly college students and young adults), has gathered weekly to serve burgers to the hundreds of partiers walking down a street full of house parties. The city has come to know and appreciate not only this ministry but also the many lives this ministry has transformed.

JESUS BURGERS IS AVAILABLE AT YOUR
FAVORITE BOOK STORE